The Power of Positive Preaching to the Saved

The Power of
Positive Preaching
to the Saved

JOHN R. BISAGNO

BROADMAN PRESS
Nashville, Tennessee

Library of Congress Catalog Card Number: 79–145978
Dewey Decimal Classification: 252
Printed in the United States of America

Preface

Some sermons look better than they sound! Few messages are powerful in both dimensions. But the sermons appearing in this volume not only read well, but they sounded great as they were preached in the pulpit of First Baptist Church, El Paso, Texas, when John Bisagno came for a revival during the summer of 1969.

Most of them are appearing here exactly as they were delivered, having been mechanically recorded and transcribed. It was a powerful week, with the moving of the Holy Spirit obvious in every service. Church members were genuinely revived and scores of people were saved.

Many question whether a sermon could ever be preached entirely on an "either-or" basis—either to Christians or to the unsaved? The primary thrust of these sermons is clearly to the church member, yet each message also contains a solid evangelistic note for those who do not know the Savior.

God blessed these sermons in our pulpit; I am confident he will bless them in this book.

Gene Garrison, Pastor
First Baptist Church
El Paso, Texas

Contents

1. Is the Bible True?   9

2. Eternal Security   23

3. The Sin unto Death   33

4. How Will You Die?   45

5. His Majesty, the Devil   57

6. The Anatomy of a Murder   69

7. The Sexual Revolution   83

8. This I Believe   99

9. The Glorification of the Believer   115

1
Is the Bible True?

Is the Bible true? Obviously, yes! "Obviously," you say? That is what I said. Of course, if you already have your mind made up, even the obvious is absurd. But I believe that if you have an open, honest, attitude toward the matter, and are willing to know the truth, I can prove to you by everything reasonable and right that this wonderful old Book we call the Bible, is indeed the Word of God. And while we are on the subject, if you have any serious doubts about his existence, you will have to admit that if I can prove to you that the Bible is God's Book, then obviously God exists.

There are many reasons why I believe the Bible to be true. Here are seven of them:

1. I believe the Bible is the Word of God because of its *presumption*. The dictionary defines presumption as a strong probability; the assumption of the credibility of certain facts from circumstantial evidence.

The sincere seeker for truth will soon realize that it is an honest assumption to begin by presuming the Bible to be the Word of God. You must begin somewhere. A man either starts by assuming that it is true or it is not true. In a court of law in America, a man is presumed innocent until proven guilty, not vice versa. I believe we can pay the same honor to this best of books. Man has always questioned: "Did I come from somewhere? Did someone create me? Is there a higher power? If there is, did he ever speak to man? If so, what did he say? Did someone write it down? Is this book we call the Bible a record of those words? If not, who has them? Why don't they share them with me?" Entirely too many questions go unanswered, when we do not begin by presuming the Bible to be the Word of God.

Darwin said, "I regret that I tossed out the possibility of evolution as a theory and gullible men gobbled it up as a fact." Voltaire on his deathbed said, "I am abandoned by God and man. I shall go to hell." Huxley said, "So, it is true, so it is true!" And died.

But what a difference in the death of the men who believed and loved the Bible. D. L. Moody said, "This is my coronation day; don't try to call me back." Charles Spurgeon, when facing death, said, "Can this be death? Why it is better than living." Dr. Amos Squire, for many years associated with Sing Sing prison said, "Ninety-seven percent of the men who come here have no faith in the Bible and no Sunday School or Bible training." Roger Babson, well-known statistician said, "I have never known a civic club that was not begun by Bible-believing people or the sons of Bible-believing parents. I have made this statement before over 400 civic clubs and have yet to be corrected." Zachary Taylor said, "It is the foundation of our Government." Dwight D. Eisenhower said, "I owe my success to the

Word of God." Dr. Warner von Braun, eminent atomic scientist, said, "I believe in Divine Creation; the Divinity of Jesus Christ and the Word of God." Graham Blaine, Jr., said, "America's greatest problem is the problem of guilt, most of which are unconfessed sins. Most people do not need psychiatrists nearly as much as they need the blood of Jesus Christ." The Bible says of itself, "Heaven and earth shall pass away, but my words shall never pass away." Two thousand times, the Bible says, "Thus saith the Lord." I cannot believe that something fabricated on 2,000 lies would not have been totally discredited by intelligent men years ago. The Bible says of itself that it is to be taught; appealed to; read; received; published; sought; searched; loved; longed for; and rejoiced in. It says that the Scriptures are inspired of God; approved of Christ; breathed by the Holy Spirit. That they are the Word of God; the book of law; the Holy Book; powerful; pure; perfect; true; timely; instructive; and comforting. I believe it is reasonable to begin by presuming the Bible to be the Word of God.

The first time that Satan approached man directly, it was at the point of the veracity of the Word of God. He did not say that God's words were not true, he merely raised the question. If he can penetrate your mind by raising a question, he will go a long way toward his goal of deceiving you.

2. I believe the Bible is the Word of God because of its *protection*. It has been cussed and discussed, analyzed and ridiculed by its friends and praised by its enemies for years. Yet it towers above every other book.

It is obvious that someone, somewhere, is protecting the Bible.

In 1907, a British colporteur was traveling through Bohemia and came upon a village where missionaries had never been. He discovered that there were no locks on the doors, for there was no crime; and no jails, for there were no theives. The entire community had been Christianized. Inquiring as to what missionaries had converted the town, he was told this story:

Several years ago in a neighboring village, a group of men were burning hundreds of Bibles in a bonfire. A charred piece of the Bible, had floated on the breeze into this community. A blacksmith and his son finding the fragments could make out only the words, "Heaven and earth shall pass away, but my words shall never pass away." They were so impressed that they went to other villages and gathered enough pieces to put together a Bible. They did not preach it nor did they teach it, but for years they just passed it around. People read it, believed its truth, accepted its Christ, and practiced its precepts. The Holy Spirit had done his work with his Word. Someone, something, somewhere is protecting the message of the Bible.

3. I believe the Bible is the Word of God, because of its *perfection*. The Bible is not really a book, it is a library of sixty-six different books. These books were written by approximately forty authors who lived a total of sixteen hundred years apart in different parts of the country, and spoke different languages. Many of them didn't even know the others existed. Yet, there is one plan of salvation; one God; one theology; one

source of redemption taught on its pages. It was written by fishermen, kings, merchants, tax collectors, rabbis, men from all walks of life. How can you explain the unity, the perfection of the finished product.

If you were to go around the world and choose sixty-six books at random in different languages on different subjects written sixteen centuries apart, what chance would you have of making one perfect book out of them?

The central theme of the Bible is Jesus Christ. It begins with Jesus Christ as the bud in Genesis that produces the flower, the finished fruit in Revelation, the coming, ruling King of kings. The Old Testament conceals Christ, the New Testament reveals Christ. The Old Testament veils Christ, the New Testament unveils Christ. The Old Testament is Christ concealed, the New Testament is Christ revealed. The Old Testament contains Christ, the New Testament explains Christ. It is, indeed, "The Jesus Book."

Suppose that from the major stone quarries of America all kinds of rocks and stones came together in one place. There was no plan, no blueprint, no order, they just showed up. Then when they were put together, there stood before your eyes the most perfect and beautiful edifice the world had ever seen. Every pole, arch, vault, doorway, buttress, precisely in place. Not a stone left out; not one too few. How could you explain the unity of the finished product? Even the most worldly skeptic would have to admit that there was one central architect who planned it all. How can you explain the finished product of the world's most beautiful and perfect book, unless there is someone who could live for sixteen hundred years, and there is no one unless there be a God and unless this Bible is his Book. How do you explain the perfection and balance of this world? This earth that is turning 23½ degrees on its axis. If a degree less, it could drop into obscurity, a degree more, and it could spin into oblivion. This earth that is so perfectly related to the moon that it gives us the seasons and makes life possible on the earth. This earth, ninety-three million miles from the sun, if a hundred miles closer would burn, or a hundred miles further would freeze us all to death. How does one explain the balance and order of the universe? The very best that science has come up with is that it just happened. These certain gases formed one day, they say, and then when everything was just right, "Boom,', out jumped this perfect world. That makes as much sense to me as saying that there was an explosion in a printing plant, and out jumped a complete unabridged dictionary.

The perfection of the Bible proves for me that its author lived sixteen hundred years and beyond and I know even more important than that, that by faith he lives within my heart.

4. I believe the Bible is the Word of God because of its *prophecy*. History is a record of events after they happen. Almost anyone can write history. But none but God could write prophecy. Prophecy is a record of events before they happen. How do you explain the fact that on page after page, the Bible predicts what will happen, when it will happen, and then it comes to pass? The Bible is replete with literally hundreds of

prophecies. The Bible prophesied the manner of destruction almost to the time of day, the destruction of city after city in early civilization. The prophecies found in this book say to the intelligent mind that somebody who knew the end from the beginning must have been at its source.

The Bible said Jesus would be born of a virgin—he was. That he would come out of Bethlehem—he did. He would work in his father's carpenter shop—he did. That he would work miracles, die on the cross, and rise the third day—All of these, he did. The Bible said one day hot and cold would come from the same hole in the wall.—Today electricity for stoves or refrigerators and hot and cold running water do come from the same hole in the wall. The Bible said horseless chariots would run four abreast on great highways of stone—Have you been on the freeways lately?

5. I believe the Bible is the Word of God because of its *perfection*. The Bible is not a book of science, it is a book of religion. It is not a Book about how go the heavens, it is a book about how to go to heaven. However, when it does deal in scientific issues it is always correct.

Science and the Bible are not in contradiction. Any time you find a supposed discrepancy between science and the Scriptures, one of two things is true. It is not really science or it is not really Scripture, you just think its Scripture. The Bible says in the last days many psuedo-scientists, falsely so-called, will arise and deceive men. There is much going by the name of science today that is not really science at all. For example: No real

scientist will ever claim a theory to be a fact. The theory
of evolution is an unproved theory, as are many other
theories called fact by so many so-called scientists. Further, any real scientist is just as interested in proving his
theory wrong as he is in proving it right.

Then too, often times, we credit the Bible with saying things that it does not really say at all. The Bible,
for example, does not say that the earth is 6,000 years
old. The Bible speaks of creative days. But translated,
the Hebrew word "day," "Yom" has many meanings
and doesn't necessarily mean a twenty-four hour period.
In Genesis 1:1, God created the earth, but 1:2 says it
fell; it was, literally it became, without form and void.
Something happened. It lay empty and impotent for
endless millenniums of years.

The Bible is not in contradiction with science as to
the order of the creation of life on this earth. Animals
existed on the earth before human life, and when
God created Adam and Eve he brought the animals,
which already existed, to them to be named. But man
was the instant creation of Almighty God.

The Bible said, "The life of the flesh is in the blood"
(Lev. 17:11). They used to drain blood and men
would die. Now, they give blood transfusions. Scientists
were wrong—the Bible was right.

The Bible says, "He hangeth the earth upon nothing"
(Job 26:7). For years, the scientist laughed and said
the earth had foundation, but now science has admitted
its error. Science was wrong—the Bible was right. They
know the earth does hang on nothing.

The Bible says, He sitteth upon the circle of the

earth. They said that the earth was flat, but now they know the earth is round. He does sit upon the circle of the earth. Science was wrong—the Bible was right.

The Bible says there is an empty spot in the Northern sky. Scientists scoffed at this. Now, they know it is true. There is an empty spot in the northern sky.

The Bible says the morning stars all sing together. Scientists said, "No." Now they know the heavenly bodies literally give off phonetic vibrations. The morning stars do sing together. Science was wrong; the Bible was right.

The Bible says there were highways in the seas. The scientists did not believe it, but now they know that you can get on the current in the sea and go against the winds. Science was wrong—the Bible was right. There are highways in the sea.

It is one thing for Moses to know the ten steps in creation, but remember, he knew their order. Who told him? Did he guess? What chance did he have of getting them in the right order. You put ten pennies in your pocket, number them 1 to 10, and pull out one. You have one chance in ten of getting number one. Put it back and start again. You have one chance in 100 of getting 1 and then 2. Put them back and start again. You have one chance in 10,000 of getting number 1, 2 and then 3. Start again. You have one chance in billions of getting number 1, 2, 3, all the way to 10 in order. Moses must have really been some kind of guesser!! Or did God tell him?

6. I believe the Bible is the Word of God because of its *power*. When people read the Bible and believe it

and do what it says, they find there a supernatural power to put away bad habits, love their neighbors, change their personality, and find peace of mind.

People have found peace and power in reading of Psalm 23, the prologue to the Gospel of John, the Sermon on the Mount that is unequaled in literature.

Recently, I asked a friend who had just returned from preaching in the Orient, to tell me of his greatest thrill. "Was it," I said, "seeing some great sporting event or a great industrial complex?" "John," he said, "it was going places where they not only had never heard the gospel, but had never heard of the gospel and seeing them immediately accept Jesus Christ as their Savior."

A psychologist said to me recently: "We have the answer to everything, but the solution to nothing. We can always find the problem. We can seldom solve it. We can take them apart, but we can't put them back together again."

I know a man named Jesus Christ who can take you apart and put you back together again. There is a supernatural power in the Bible and in its message.

7. I believe the Bible is the Word of God because of its *presentation*. Because of the message it presents. Charles Darwin created a great deal of controversy with his book *The Origin of the Species*. Frankly, I am little concerned with the origin of the species. But I am greatly interested in the destiny of the species. What am I here for? Where am I going to go? How am I supposed to get there? If there is no God, no hereafter, no judgment, I haven't missed much after all. I am very happy in this life, but if you do not believe it, and

I am right and you are wrong, you have missed everything!!! If you make a mistake, be sure you make it on the right side.

The Bible is the world's only authoritative message as to the origin and destiny of man. Its simple, clear-cut message is this: A loving God gives man the privilege of enjoying the blessings and benefits of voluntarily choosing to serve and honor him.

But the self-willed man chooses not to do so. This loving God went a step further and presented redemption for man, by sending his Son, Jesus Christ, to die for our sins. And all who receive him may live in peace and in fellowship with God.

In 1963, the famous *Mona Lisa* was brought to America for display. A reporter asked one of the marines guarding the famed portrait, "What was the one most consistent comment made by Americans who viewed the *Mona Lisa?*" Do you know what we said the most often? "So, that is the famous *Mona Lisa* I have heard so much about. That thing—ha!! I don't see what is so hot about that."

Remember this. The *Mona Lisa* has withstood the test of time. When you view the *Mona Lisa*, it is not on trial, you are. Your aesthetic values, your appreciation, you are on trial.

When you view the word of God, its not on trial—you are. It has stood the test of the ages. It will be the Book of Books when the writings of men have passed into the obscurity of literary limbo.

The Bible is a mirror, reflecting the glories of God, the sinfulness of man, and the Jesus Christ to meet that need. Don't throw stones. Accept your need. Receive Jesus, live and die by the Word of God.

When Sir Walter Scott lay dying, he cried, "Bring me the Book." His nephew said, "Which book sir?" And Scott replied, "Young man, there is but one book, the Bible."

2
Eternal Security

Can a man who has accepted Jesus Christ as his personal Savior and been born again by the spirit of God ever be lost? By every rule in the book, it would seem that he could indeed. From observation, from experience, from our own reasoning, everything would point to it. But to find our authoritative answers to this and every controversial issue, we need to go by the rules of the real book—the Bible. As in most controversial issues, it is difficult to give consideration to the issue with an open mind. However, I am going to ask you to be very unbiased as you read these pages on why I believe that a man who has once been genuinely born of the Spirit of God can never again so sin as to lose his salvation.

To the layman, religion would seem to be a very confusing matter. Ask one hundred people how to be saved, and you will probably get one hundred different answers. Some will say, it is by faith. Others, by holding out faithful; by baptism; by confirmation; by church membership. Still others will deny life after death, or God's relationship to man in this life, and will deny that there is such a thing as salvation. Confusing? Not really. For there are, after all, not hundreds of ideas as to how to be saved, but only two. What every denomination believes about how to get from here to heaven, can be boiled down to one simple question: Is salvation by grace or is it by works? Grace, plus works, is not grace at all, but works. It is the oldest question in theology. It is the heart of the matter. It is the one thing that really counts. The answer can be found in Ephesians 2:8–9: "For by grace are ye saved through faith; and that not of yourselves: it is the gift of God: not of works, lest any man should boast." Let there be no misunderstanding, works are the important product of salvation. The imperative result of salvation. Verse 10 continues to tell us that unless a life produces good work, there has been no new birth.

Works are certainly the outward proof of salvation, and without them there has been no salvation; no changed life; no fruits, no salvation. One may say, "I was saved by grace, but I must keep working, or I will not get to heaven." Wrong! What do you mean, "saved?" I wouldn't give two cents for a salvation that did not get me out of hell and get me into heaven. If it doesn't do that, it is not salvation, at all. It is merely religion. What has it saved you from? What has it saved you to. By salvation, I mean that I finally arrive at my home in heaven; and if I get 99 percent of the way and end up missing it, it didn't do me any good at all, now did it?

One can drown three feet from the shore and be just as dead as though he had drowned in the middle of the Atlantic Ocean. The Bible is ultimate and final, definitely, completely clear on the point as to how one is saved. Believe on the Lord, Jesus Christ, and thou shalt be saved. All of our righteousness is as filthy rags, he only accepts his shed blood. Only his grace is sufficient. It is, indeed, by grace through faith, not of ourselves, that men are saved!

Many argue that this freedom of grace is a license to sin. But such is not the case at all. The fact that my wife trusts me does not encourage me to run around, it encourages my faithfulness. The man who says, "If I believed that, I would do what I wanted to," if he really means it, has probably never been saved at all.

The idea of one's salvation being earned and deserved by his good works, deters the salvation of the lost. How many have rejected salvation by saying, "I just can't live," never realizing that it is Christ in them that does the living. Many will give up at the first failure, thinking they have lost their salvation and delight Satan.

Here is the heart of it all—"Just as I am, without one plea, but that thy blood was shed for me. Oh, Lamb of God, I come." "Amazing grace, how sweet the sound, that saved a wretch like me."

There is no greater encouragement of my salvation; no stronger motivation than that he that hath begun a good work in me and will perform it until the day of Jesus Christ. For by grace are ye saved through faith!!

So, the heart of the matter, the ultimate destiny of the soul who trusts in Christ, the eternal security of the believer, how he will finish his salvation is *how was it begun?* It all boils down to this. Is it by grace or by works? If by works, we can fail. For if we do not work hard enough, we can lose it. But if by grace, then the burden, the responsibility, the victory, the price is his. If the blood of Christ does not cleanse from all sin, if his grace is not sufficient for every sin, and if any sin can separate us from a loving God, then I raise the question, "How many sins does it take to make you lost?" You might say, "Well, if one sins badly enough, he will lose his salvation." How bad is bad enough? I suppose if a man got drunk and died, he would be lost. If it takes a man ten bottles of beer to get drunk, and he drinks nine and a half and dies, does he go to hell or to heaven? Jesus said, "He who thinks, is guilty." He who desires in his heart has committed the act. So, at what point does one lose his salvation, the desire or the act?

It is not grace plus works. You must answer my question. You must settle it once and for all! The question of eternal security is as simple as this: Are we saved by grace or by works?" If one is saved by works, then go right ahead and work. You have no need of salvation. You have no need of grace. You have no need of the righteousness of a holy God. You have no need of mercy, no need of blood. You can make it by yourself. Go ahead—lots of luck! You'll need it!

There are many verses in the Bible that are used as so called proof texts to try to show that a man having been saved can lose his salvation. In every case, they are taken out of context and misunderstood. Let us examine a few.

First John 3:9, "Whosoever is born of God does not commit sin," is one such verse. The word "commit" simply means to give a committal to. When someone is committed to a mental hospital, they are given over to the hospital for their treatment and care. One who is born of God may stumble and fall, but his new nature will not long stay in the hogpen of sin. It is not fitting. He finds it distasteful. He now has a new and different nature and will not give a committal over to the old "hogpen life." When a man is really born of the Spirit of God, everytime he wants to get drunk, he probably will, but the point is, he won't want to any more. He has a new heart with new desires. This does not mean he will never be tempted and sin again, but when he does he will not give a committal over to the old way of life. He simply cannot, it is not possible. His new nature will not allow him. He will not, having been born of God, again give a committal back over to sin. If he does, he was never born of God. It is that simple.

Galatians 5:4 is another misunderstood verse. "Ye are fallen from grace." When you pick those words out of a middle of a chapter, it looks like a man can lose his salvation, because the verse says, "Ye are fallen from grace." But is this what it means? Not at all. There are over 1,000 words, 149 verses, 6 chapters in the book of Galatians that deal exclusively with one question: "Should a man who has been saved by the grace of God try to go back and mix the Jewish law with his Christian grace and go back to a lower plane of reason; go back under the law which was merely a teacher to bring him to Christ in the first place?"

The Galatian people to whom Paul was writing, were real Christians! They were so alive and so related to

God that they just couldn't do enough. They said, "Let's keep on going to prayer meeting; let's keep on reading the Bible; but let's also go back and add the Jewish law and fast and add special days to our new way of life." Paul says, "Are you going to leave college and go back to kindergarten by going back under the law? You are slipping from that high calling in Jesus, you are going backward, rather than forward. Back to the law which was on a schoolmaster to bring you to the grace that is in Christ Jesus."

Salvation does not ask the question, can a man be saved and then lost, but now having received salvation, which is the best road to take of Christian growth? It is certainly not by leaving the college of grace and going back to the kindergarten of the Jewish Law.

Philippians 2:12–13 tells us to work out our own salvation with fear and trembling, but quickly adds, "For it is God that worketh in you both to will and to do of his good pleasure." This, too, is often misunderstood. Paul went to Philippi and other cities preaching the gospel; winning converts; organizing and establishing churches. After Paul's leaving them, there arose problems peculiar to each new church. The Philipians were discouraged. Many were giving up. Many were discouraged. "Paul has left us," they said. "What shall we do?" Paul told them, "Now that you have been saved, get to work. You don't have Paul, but you have God. He is in you. He is with you, not only to give you the desire to work, but the ability to do it as well!"

What about the individual who on the outside seems to have a genuine experience with God, but then falters and dies in the same condition in which he began. This seems to be the unanswerable question, but it is easily understood and answered in the New Testament.

First, there is the possibility that he never was saved at all. He had an emotional experience; came forward; joined the church, but never came to Christ, who said, "Him that cometh to me I will in no wise cast out" (John 6:37). So, after an experience that is merely an experience and not an experience with God, he goes back to the old ways in a few weeks. He did not lose his salvation, he simply never had it in the first place.

There is the second possibility that the individual will be saved and then backslide. God will correct and chastize him and he will return to the Lord.

The third possibility is that he was truly saved, but got away from God, was corrected but would not repent. He will be prematurely taken out of the world. But though he loses his life, he does not lose his salvation! It is called, "The sin unto death" and is found in 1 Corinthians 5:1–15 and elsewhere. It tells of a man living in adultery. His church was instructed to turn him over to Satan. He was killed, taken home prematurely, but his spirit was still saved. His soul was safe.

There are other illustrations of this in the Bible. Drunkenness at the Lord's Supper table also leads to the sin unto death. When the backslider refuses to return to his Lord, he loses his life, but not his salvation.

Let us suppose that one could lose his salvation. What would he have to do to regain it? Simply fall down and beg for forgiveness and be converted a second time? Not so!! Hebrews 6:4–6 states about such a case. If a man, once saved, could fall away, it would be impossible to ever restore him. Why? Because to provide for the salvation of the world, certain things must happen. Jesus Christ must live a perfect life, die on the cross and be raised from the dead. If you could so sin as to undo all that he did before, you could never be saved again. Jesus would have to do all of that again. But thank God he will never come from heaven again to die, only to reign. He will never again shed his blood. He will never be crucified a second time. There was sufficient righteousness; sufficient power; in that first perfect life; to cover for all my sin!!

How long does everlasting life last? A week? A month? A year? How long? For ever! I could disinherit my children; change their names; hate them; turn on them; reject them; break all fellowship with them; but I can never break the relationship. They are my children and they will always be. Fellowship can be broken, relationship cannot.

A careful study of Romans 8:29–31,35–39 will give a panoramic sweep of the world. From predestination to glorification. From the foundation of this world, there is nothing that can separate us from God.

Yes, I admit that by reasoning, it is hard to comprehend, but when I realize that God, having foreknown me, did predestinate me to be conformed to the image of his Son, and nothing shall separate me from the final accomplishment of that fact, then I cry with the songwriter of old, "Amazing grace how sweet the sound that saved a wretch like me." It is hard for me to understand why he could keep me saved, but there is one thing, far more difficult for me to comprehend more than that, how he could have ever saved me in the first place!

3
The Sin Unto Death

"If any man see his brother sin a sin which is not unto death, he shall ask, and he shall give him life for them that sin not unto death. There is a sin unto death; I do not say that he shall pray for it. All unrighteousness is sin: and there is a sin not unto death" (1 John 5:16–17).

The question of once saved, always saved, and what happens to the backslider is one of the most controversial in the world. However, the Bible seems to me very clear at this point. There are only three possibilities as to the man who says he is saved, begins well, and ends up wrong. Remember, however, that you cannot judge whether he was ever saved or not. Man looks on the outside, but only God looks on the heart. And so the argument that you once knew a man who was saved and then died in a backslidden condition does not really hold water at all. Because you don't know whether or not he was ever truly saved in the first place.

But as to the original question, there are three possibilities. Number one, there is the possibility that the man was never saved at all. He is a liar, a hypocrite, who just pretended to be saved but was never really saved at all. He will go to hell. Not because he lost salvation, but because he never had it in the first place.

There is the second possibility that a man will be saved and then he will backslide, and God will chastise him and correct him and bring him back. The Bible says that God scourges and corrects every son whom he receives. You may know whether you have really been born again by whether God corrects you when you do wrong. "For if ye are without chastisement, then are ye bastards, and not sons, illegitimate and not Sons of God at all." But if you are chastised when you sin, you may be sure that you are a son of God. And so the second possibility is that one will really be saved, will backslide and that God will correct him and chastise him for his own good and bring him back.

Then there is the third possibility which we shall consider. That is the possibility of the sin unto death. That a man will get so far away from God that when God reproves him he will not repent and God will prematurely take him out of this life that he may still go to heaven.

In 1 John 5:16–17, we find our text. Let's look at it again. "If any man see his brother . . ." The word "brother" in the Bible means Christian brother, a saved man, a brother in Christ. "If any man see his brother sin a sin that is not unto death, he shall ask, and he shall give him life." In other words, you can pray for the backslidden brother's sins under certain conditions. But there is one kind of sin that a brother commits that it is useless to pray for. It is the sin unto death. This is not the unpardonable sin. The unpardonable sin is the sinner resisting the Holy Spirit's call so long that he is hardened in his sins, and he dies and goes to hell, as an unsaved person. A Christian cannot commit any unpardonable sin. God may, however, take the Christian prematurely out of this world. He will be taken physically, but his soul will still be saved as we shall see in the Scriptures.

And so if you see your backslidden brother sin most sins, pray for him. But there is one kind of sin, the sin unto death, that a Christian can commit, that when he gets far enough away from God, God says forget it, it's useless, don't pray for him. He has committed the sin unto death. God will take him prematurely from the world that his influence may not count against Him.

Several times the Bible records incidents of the sin unto death. The first we shall consider is in 1 Corinthians 5. You will remember that the Corinthian church was the one with which the apostle Paul had the most trouble in all of the New Testament. They were a wild and woolly bunch to be sure. There were always problems of immorality, drunkness, and licentiousness, and on and on. In the fifth chapter, Paul writing to the Corinthians says, "It is a common fact that immorality goes on in your midst." And he says, "The kind that is not so much as named among the Gentiles." In other words, even the heathen, the unsaved wouldn't do what you are doing. And then he spelled out specifically what it was that they were doing. "That one should have his father's wife." In other words there was some one in the church of Corinth living in open adultery either with his mother, his step-mother, or his mother-in-law. And he adds, "You are puffed up, you're bragging about it. You haven't mourned, you haven't done anything about it that this one that has done the deed might be taken away from you." Paul believed in old-fashioned church discipline. But he goes on to say, "Whether you judge or not, I've judged, and by the Spirit of God I'm going to tell you what you ought to do." Listen to 1 Corinthians 5:4. "In the name of our Lord Jesus Christ, when ye are gathered together, and my spirit. . . ." Next Sunday, and the next time you get together, here's what to do. "Deliver such an one unto satan for the destruction of the flesh, that the spirit may be saved in the day of the Lord Jesus." He said to turn him over to the devil. Let the devil kill him, get him out of the world, physically kill him that his spirit, his soul might still be saved.

You see, he commits the sin unto death. God gets rid of him and takes him prematurely on to heaven, because he is bringing reproach on the name of Christ. The enemies of God are blaspheming and the cause of Christ is suffering because of him.

Now, he doesn't go to hell, he still goes to heaven. He doesn't lose his salvation, but he is killed. God takes him out of the world prematurely that his spirit still might be saved in the day of the Lord Jesus Christ.

Some may say, "That means turn him over to Satan so that Satan can beat him around a little bit and get some of the sin out of him." Listen, Satan never cooperated with God to do anything good for him, and getting the sin out of him and getting him to be better and rededicate his life would have been good for him.

No, Satan wouldn't cooperate in that. He turned him over to Satan for the ultimate destruction of the flesh, to destroy him, to kill him, that his spirit still might be saved in the day of the Lord Jesus.

Many years ago a famous preacher who was very liberal divorced his wife and married the wife of one of his deacons. The deacon married the preacher's wife. All four of them swapped partners, and continued to run around together and be friends. Many friends went to them and told them they were bringing reproach on the name of Christ, and begged them to break up their mocking, adulterous relationship. They laughed at them and persisted in their sin. Within a few months, the four of them crashed in a plane at a major airport and were instantly killed. I believe they committed the sin unto death. You cannot go on and on blaspheming God and bringing reproach on the name of Christ as a backslidden preacher or a backslidden Christian. God will ultimately bring you to the sin unto death. He will get you out of the way that his work might go on. People may not endlessly blaspheme his name. He will kill you if necessary. Your soul will still be saved, so as by fire. By the skin of your teeth, you will go to heaven. But you will have no rewards. Extreme sexual sins may lead to the sin unto death.

The second incident of the sin unto death is recorded in the book of Acts. There in the fifth chapter beginning in the first verse, the Bible tells us of two people named Ananias and Sapphira. There was a great revival going on in their community. People were selling all of their goods, lands and properties in order to have money for the work of the Lord. Ananias and Sapphira were Christians. They were leaders in the church, and so the pressure was on. They had to make a good show. They had to make it appear as though they too were dedicated. But they were not. They made an agreement that they would sell the land and keep part of the money and say that they only sold it for so much when in reality they had sold it for much more. They lied to the Holy Spirit. They had kept back part of the price of commitment. They pretended to be something that they were not. They committed the sin unto to death.

Peter said, "Ananias and Sapphira why has Satan filled thine heart to lie to the Holy Spirit? You didn't have to give the land. God doesn't want your dedication by constraint, he wants it willingly. While it remained, was it not yours to keep or to sell? Why have you conceived this thing in your heart?" The Bible says out of the abundance of the heart a man speaks. The heart is desperately wicked; who can know it. Out of the heart proceeds the issues of life. What they did was a result of what they were in their hearts. They were hypocrites, they were liars. They lied through their mouths because they were liars in their hearts. They were saved, but they had a cheap, shallow kind of dedication to Jesus Christ. Peter said, "Thou has not lied unto men, but unto God" (Acts 5:4). And the Bible says that hearing these things they fell down dead and gave up the ghost. Two young men came in, carried them out and buried them.

Ananias and Sapphira were church leaders, but their lives were hypocritical. They lied to God. They pretended to be one thing, but were another. And finally the cup of divine indignation was filled to the brim and God was so disgusted that he killed them and got them out of the world.

You had better be careful if you are a leader in church. To whom much is given much is required. If your life is a lie to the Holy Spirit, you may be on the verge of committing the sin unto death.

The third incidence of the sin unto death is unworthily handling of the things of God. The Bible tells us also in the book of 1 Corinthians that some people were getting drunk at the Lord's Supper table. They were taking the vessels of God and handling them unworthily. The Bible says, "For this cause, the cause of getting drunk at the Lord's Supper table, unworthily handling the things of God, desecrating the vessels of God, many are sick among you and many even sleep." Actual physical maladies were coming upon them.

You know of course that sleep in the Bible means death. In other words, for this cause some were sick and some were even dead.

If you are unworthily handling the things of God, taking the talents, the bread, the vehicles, the vessels of God, the possessions, the opportunities that God has given you, and you are using them as an occasion to sin, using them for an opportunity for sin rather than for sanctification to the Savior, then you are on the verge of committing the sin unto death, and I urge you to get right with God. If you teach a class, pass out bulletins, sing in a choir, or discharge any spiritual responsibility, you are especially required to be clean.

There is a fourth incident in the Word of God of the sin unto death. You will recall that the Scriptures tell us in 2 Peter 3:16, that they were perverting the Scriptures to justify their own sins. And that they did so to their own destruction. Here the Bible tells us that men wrested or twisted the Scriptures to justify their sins. It is possible for a man to so pervert the Word of God and twist what it says to justify what he is that God gets disgusted with him and kills him.

I cannot tell you how many ridiculous arguments I have heard to justify people's sins. I have heard people try to justify everything from stealing God's tithe to murder with the Bible. Twisting and perverting all out of shape what the Bible obviously says about sins in efforts to justify their own backslidden condition.

I have heard them laugh and say, "You know what we Baptists believe, once saved always saved, ha, ha, ha!" As though God thought their backslidden condition were funny. Listen, my friend, God doesn't think your backsliding is funny. We sing the little song, "Though it makes him sad to see the way we live, he'll always say, I forgive." Untrue! There comes a time when God won't forgive. God says, "I want 10 percent." And we give God 1 percent and go laughing on our way. God says, "I want one day in seven." America gives God none and laughs. He says, "I want your heart, I want your life." But man takes his heart and his life as though they were his, he takes his body as though he owned it, he blasphemes God, lives like the devil, and laughs in the face of God. I warn you that you can't get away with that continually. I urge you to realize that in your backslidden condition you may be flirting with death.

Oh yes, you will be saved, though as by fire, by the very skin of your teeth. But God may take some of you prematurely as he did Ananias and Sapphira, or as the man living in incest or the one that twisted the Scriptures to justify his own sins. As he took those that were getting drunk at the Lord's supper table, so may he take you. You too, could commit the sin unto death.

You say, "Preacher, what can I do about it?" Thank God there's good news for you. The Bible says if we confess our sins, he is faithful and just to forgive us our sins and cleanse us from all unrighteousness. The blood of Jesus Christ, His son, cleanses us from every sin.

4
How Will You Die?

Several years ago I went to Los Angeles to hold a revival. One night the service was out early and the pastor and I decided to go to see the Dodgers play ball. We arrived about the seventh inning and sat on the top row, three balconies above the ground. A fly ball came my way and I reached over to grab it and nearly fell out and killed myself. On the way home as we were laughing about it, I began to think, Wouldn't that make some headline back in my hometown? "Local preacher goes to California to hold a revival and falls out of baseball stadium and breaks his neck."

Later that night the thought occurred: I wonder what the paper will say. I wonder how I will die?

I want to ask you that question: How will you die? Oh, I don't mean in an automobile accident, or by natural causes, or by a heart attack, what I mean is in what condition will you die? What spiritual state will your life be in when you die and go to meet God? I can tell you one thing for sure, you'll die just exactly as you have lived.

I remind you that in this day in which so many people die in hospitals, there are very few deathbed repentances. People are kept under such heavy sedation, that there is very little chance that you will have the opportunity to repent on your deathbed.

You say, "Preacher, don't talk about death. Don't try to scare me. All right, I'll make you a promise. You promise me you'll never die, and I promise you I'll never talk about death. Ah, but you're going to die. Death is certain. Eternity is certain. Hell is moving, deathbeds are coming. And today is the day of salvation. How will you die?

Let us go through the Word of God and look at some men to see how they died.

First of all, *the rich man died unprepared*. You remember the story in Luke. Jesus tells us of a rich man and a poor man. The poor man died and went to heaven, not because he was poor, but because he was saved. The rich man died and went to hell, not because he was rich, but because he was lost. "And in hell," the Bible says, "he experienced awful, undescribable and endless torment." What a shame for a man to go to hell, when he has had every opportunity. I can imagine the *Jerusalem Gazette* must have headlined the news that a rich and famous man is now dead. Little did they know that he was screaming in the flames of hell.

Oh, he had probably made every earthly provision. He must have had a grand funeral. The heads of state probably came from near and far to pay homage to this great man. But he was in hell. The couriers surely came night after night, bearing beautiful baskets of fruit and food to the home and bedecking his casket with flowers. But he was in hell. The insurance man perhaps came and told his wife of the hundreds of thousands of dollars that he had left to her. How very happy that must have made her. But he was in hell. His sons probably had provision for the finest education. His wife was well taken care of. The estate was paid for. Everything was in readiness for his death. He had prepared everything but the one thing that really counts, his soul's salvation. And he was in hell.

What an awful shame to have a burial policy, to have an insurance policy, to have every provision, to take care of your children, and yet to die, unprepared in the thing that really matters the most. The rich man died unprepared.

Now, there is another man in the Bible to whom I want us to give our consideration. You will remember him. His name is Ananias. *Ananias died unclean.* Pretending to be something that he was not, his life was a hypocrisy. God got enough of him, God became tired. He killed him and took his life. Ananias died. Oh, yes, he went to heaven, but he was ashamed, he was embarrassed. He died prematurely. He was not yet ready to meet God. The Bible says, "Prepare to meet thy God" (Amos 4:12). And that verse goes for the Christian as well as the unsaved.

Christian friend, are you ready to meet God? Is your life clean, or are there sins locked up in the secret corners of your heart, things that no one knows; unconfessed sins piled up between you and God for years? David said, "If I regard iniquity in my heart the Lord will not hear me" (Ps. 66:18). That word "regard" means to retain. If you have a high regard for some secret unconfessed sin and are retaining it in your heart, I warn you, your life is unclean. And when you die, you will stand before God, embarrassed, unclean, not ready to meet the Lord.

Now there is a third man in the Bible. Just as the rich man died unprepared, and as Ananias died unclean, you will, of course, remember Judas. I suggest to you that *Judas died unfaithful*. I do not believe that Judas was ever saved. He did not lose his salvation. He was a devil from the beginning. He went to hell not because he lost it, but because he never had it. He was the son of perdition. God knew that he was going to go to hell from the beginning.

You say, "Preacher, I don't understand that. Why did Jesus choose Judas?" I don't know. But I have a greater question than that. I have something far more difficult to comprehend than that. That is why did Jesus choose me? And why did he choose you?

Most people have a gross misconception of Judas. I do not think that Judas was a sly crook who sneaked in planning to rob, and cheat and steal. I believe that Judas was an enterprising young businessman.

When Jesus first came to Jerusalem, he came in triumph. He talked of the kingdom of God coming in glory and power. And most people thought that he was talking about a physical kingdom. To the very end the disciples were saying, "Will thou at this time restore the kingdom to Israel?" They still thought it was a physical kingdom after the resurrection. Many of them still misunderstood what Jesus was trying to say.

One woman came and said, "Lord let one of my sons be first vice-president and sit on your right hand, and let the other one be second vice-president and sit on your left hand." I can imagine that impetuous Peter must have come and said, "Lord, let me organize a navy." Another, "I'll start an army." Another, "I'll keep the books." Another, "I'll be in charge of enlisting." Over and over again they thought it was to be a physical kingdom.

When Judas saw the crowds and the power of God in Christ, he thought it would be a good business venture. And so he said, "Lord, I'll be treasurer, I'll keep the money." And Judas was like so many of us. While it was popular to follow Christ, while it was great to be a Christian, while the crowds were coming, while the revival was on, everything was great. But one day, Jesus began talking about dying. He started talking about a cross, and suffering and sacrifice. And Judas said, "Wait a minute, I hadn't bargained on any of that. I'm going to get out." And while he was getting out, he decided to get all he could out of it. So, he sold Jesus for thirty pieces of silver. Later his conscience so disturbed him that he flung the money at the feet of the Jews and went out and hanged himself. You say, "How awful he was." The very word "Judas" has a connotation that blisters the tongue of decent men. But how many of us are Judases tonight?

The evangelist came, the crowds came, the preaching was marvelous, the singing was out of this world. The preacher talked about the love of God, the benefits of the gospel, the blessing of heaven, the grace of

God, the freeness of salvation, and you came down and said, "Yes, I'll take Christ." But then the revival was over, then the evangelist left town. Then Wednesday night came and the crowd went down to a handful of folks. The preacher talked about witnessing, tithing, and service for Christ. And you said, "Wait a minute, I didn't plan on any of that," and you backslide and go away! Some of us like Judas are going to die, unfaithful.

But there is a fourth man in the Bible that thrills the heart. You recall that his name was Stephen. The Bible tells us that *Stephen died unafraid.* Thank God for Stephen. This deacon was doing what deacons are supposed to do. He was out on the street corner spreading the gospel. God did not call deacons to wait on tables. God called deacons to take care of the murmurings and the problems that arose because the tables were not being waited on. In other words it is the job of the deacon to keep things running smoothly. To keep problems down, to keep harmony in the church, to keep people off the preacher's back, to keep people from griping. To keep a sweet atmosphere so that the preacher can give his life and ministry to reading the Word of God, praying, visiting, and preaching. This deacon, thank God, had done all of these things. He was out on the street corner, helping the preacher evangelize, helping spread the Word of God. He told the Pharisees that they had nailed Jesus to the cross, and they ran on him and gnashed him with their teeth and stoned him to death. And Stephen, thank God, unafraid, didn't cow and coward in the face of opposition. He died looking in the face of God, smiling, blood running down his face, his bones broken and his head crushed. But the Bible says that he saw Jesus standing at the right hand of God.

Only twice is Jesus recorded in the Word of God as standing. Once in Revelation 3:20, "Behold, I stand at the door and knock." He so wants you to be saved that he stands in honor of the sinner who comes to him. But thank God he also stands in honor of the saint that lives a great life and comes home to him, dying the death of the persecuted. This man died unafraid.

You say you would like to die like that. But wait a minute. If you can't live for Jesus on the job, if you can't dare to be different in the high school, in the home, in the office, wherever you are, then you won't be able to die for him like that. Thank God Stephen died unafraid.

There is a fifth man in the Bible that I want us to look at briefly. His name is Saul of Tarsus. We call him Paul, the great writer of most of the New Testament. And as the rich man died unprepared, as Ananias died unclean, as Judas died unfaithful, and Stephen died unafraid, *Paul died unashamed.*

Now, for you to say that you are unashamed of Jesus is one thing, but for him to say it is somthing else. Schooled in the finest schools, raised at the feet of Gamaliel, who along with Nicodemus was one of the three greatest Jewish rabbis of all time, Paul had every reason to glory in himself.

Those early Christians were not living in beautiful

churches with stained-glass windows, where it was popular to go to church. The Christians lived in catacombs, they were the discards, the rejects, the second-class citizen. They had to meet secretely by night. They were hated and persecuted. The followers of "The Way" were thought to be ignorant and unlearned.

And yet this great citadel of knowledge, this great giant of intellectualism, this great mind, said, "God, forbid that I should glory save in the cross of our Lord Jesus Christ." And when he died they came to him and they ridiculed him, they laughed at him; but he stood by the cross.

I see the apostle Paul in a dank, dark dungeon. He hears the snitch, snitch, snitch, of steel against steel, as he asks the guard, "What's that noise?" He says, "They are sharpening the sword, Jew, they are getting ready to cut your head off in the morning." The apostle Paul sees the rats running around the dungeon. He feels his hands chained to the cold wall. The drip, drip of the water on his back, and the stench and the filth. He is almost on the verge of going back. What is the use of it? And he turns to his writer and says, "Take the pen," and he writes again to young Timothy and says, "I've made a mistake. I've chosen wrong. It's not worth it. Go back to your wife and kids, forget following Jesus." Is that what he does? No, of course not. A thousand times no. Listen, "I charge thee therefore before God, and the Lord Jesus Christ, who shall judge the quick and the dead at his appearing and his kingdom. Preach the word; be instant in season, out of season; reprove, rebuke, exhort with all longsuffering and doctrine. For the time will come when they will not endure sound doctrine. But after their own lusts shall they heap to themselves teachers, having itching ears; and they shall turn away their ears from the truth, and shall be turned unto fables. But watch thou in all things, endure afflictions, do the work of an evangelist, make full proof of thy ministry. For I am now ready to be offered, and the time of my departure is at hand. I have fought a good fight, I have finished my course, I have kept the faith: Henceforth there is laid up for me a crown of righteousness, which the Lord, the righteous judge, shall give me at that day . . . unto all them also that love his appearing" (2 Tim. 4:1–8) .

Listen to it. Isn't it wonderful? Thank God that this man Paul, this giant of the ages died unashamed.

And how will you die? I can answer that question very simply for you. You will die exactly as you have lived. I urge you to order your life, to make things right with God, to set up the condition of your heart exactly as you will want it to be when you die and face God. Live so that you will be ready to die. And then you will be ready to live.

5
His Majesty, the Devil

"How art thou fallen from heaven, O Lucifer, son of the morning! How art thou cut down to the ground, which didst weaken the nations! For thou hast said in thine heart, I will ascend into heaven, I will exalt my throne above the stars of God: I will sit also upon the mount of the congregation, in the sides of the north: I will ascend above the heights of the clouds; I will be like the most High. Yet thou shalt be brought down to hell, to the sides of the pit" (Isaiah 14:12–15).

Do you believe in the devil? Unfortunately, there are many people who believe that it is a sign of their superior intelligence to disbelieve in the reality of a literal, personal devil. I want to ask you, however, to remember five things. The definiteness of the devil; the dethronement of the devil; the deception of the devil; the destruction of the devil; and finally the defense against the devil.

First consider the *definiteness of the devil*. If you believe the Bible, you must believe in the devil. Perhaps if you have never wrestled with temptation until your blood raced with the wind, you do not believe in a personal devil. Perhaps if you've never stepped out on faith and really tried to live for Christ, the devil knows you are a dead dog, and he's got you right where he wants you, so he's leaving you alone. If that is your condition you probably do not believe in a literal, personal devil.

The Bible tells us, however, that Satan actually exists. He was cast out of heaven, was resisted by Job, Jesus, the disciples, and will be cast into hell. The Bible says he walks, he talks, he lies, he flatters, he kills, he tempts, he destroys, he quotes the Scriptures. The Bible says that he is a roaring lion, a wolf, a fowl, a prowler, a beast, a sower of tares. The Bible calls him terrible, fierce, deceitful, powerful, Beelzabub, Satan, Lucifer, a liar, the devil. Over and over again the Bible tells us of the reality of a literal, personal devil.

When I see a wrist watch, I know that watch had a maker. When I see the result, I must acknowledge the cause. And when I look at the suffering, the temptation, the disease, the sin, the poverty, the ignorance, the iniquity of a lost world, and know that the God that made this world is not the author of confusion and is not the author of sin, it becomes obvious to me that someone has been tampering with God's perfect plan. That someone is his majesty, the devil.

The Bible says, "Be sober, be vigilant; for your adversary the devil, as a roaring lion, walketh about, seeking whom he may devour" (1 Pet. 5:8). I have never seen Abraham Lincoln or Thomas Jefferson, but I believe that they lived, because I've seen the results of their work. And I've seen the result of what Satan has done.

Years ago a camel driver was taking a caravan of camels across the desert. The next day he said to the people, "We had intruders in the area last night." They asked "How did you know? We didn't see anyone, and we didn't hear anyone." And he responded, "Because I see their tracks in the sand."

Go with me to the hospitals, the asylums, the bars, and the joints, look at the result of sin and on every hand you will see the tracks of Satan.

You say you believe it to be a sign of your superior intelligence to disbelieve the devil? Then my friend, you are the biggest, walking, talking, living proof of the reality of the devil in the world. The devil has you right where he wants you! He is the father of lies, the master of deceit! And he wants nothing more than to get you to believe that he does not exist. If you believe that, you are the class "A" exhibit of the power of his work.

Number two consider the *dethronement of the devil*. From whence did Satan come? The Bible calls him Satan, Lucifer, the devil, and many other names. But he is only one person. The devil is not omnipotent. He does not have all power. He has to go before God as with Job before he can touch a single heart, a single person. Nor is he omnipresent! He is not everywhere at once. He said to God, "I have been walking to and fro, up and down the land!" Now, the devil has many fallen angels, imps, demons, who assist him in his work, but he cannot be everywhere at once. He can only be at one place at a time. He is not omnipresent as is our heavenly father.

Many people ask, "Why did God make sin and why did God make the devil?" God didn't make sin and God didn't make the devil. God created Lucifer and Lucifer made himself the devil. It appears from the fourteenth chapter of Isaiah that God had an angelic society in heaven. Over this society there seemed to be the most powerful, the most intelligent, and most beautiful of all created beings! His name was Lucifer, "son of the morning." After endless centuries and countless ages, Lucifer began to be dissatisfied with doing the will of God. And the first time that he put those two words, "I" and "will" back to back, instead of "Thy will be done," sin began.

Pride entered Lucifer's heart, and seven times in the fourteenth chapter of Isaiah, the Bible records that Lucifer said, "I will." "I will ascend into heaven, I will exalt my throne above the stars of God: I will sit also upon the mount of the congregation . . . I will ascend above the heights of the clouds; I will be like the most High" (Isa. 14:13–14). When Satan said, "I will" sin began. But sin cannot exist in the presence of God. And Satan was banished from heaven. It appears, however, that the banishment did not take place till after a rebellious war in heaven. Apparently one third of the angels sided with Lucifer. The result was a foregone conclusion. They were banished from God's presence in heaven and came to the earth. Remember, God did not make the devil! God made Lucifer, Lucifer made himself the devil, and the devil started sin.

Third, consider the *deception of the devil*. Having been banished from heaven, Satan now has a plan and a program. He still hates God, he still wants to run the universe, he still wants to overthrow God. But now, banished from God, he cannot get directly at God, he cannot fight directly with him to carry on his rebellious war and his iniquitous plan, so he comes to the earth, God's chief creation, and here through God's beloved creature, man, Satan continues his war against God, through man. Satan knows that Jesus is going to come from heaven and carry the war against him. He knows his days are numbered, and he knows ultimately that he is going to be destroyed and cast into the lake of fire. But until that time he is going to try to overthrow God.

He knows that Jesus Christ is not going to come in the form of a plant or an animal. He is coming in the form of a human being. He is coming in the form of a man. And so Satan goes to the federal head of the race, and he spoils Adam and Eve with sin. He thinks in doing so that he will be able to pollute the human race and Jesus will not be able to be born. But God foreshadowing the coming of Christ and his death on the cross slays a lamb and atones for man's sins. From the beginning Satan seems to make one fatal mistake. He seems to forget that it was not through his life, but through his death, through the shed blood of the cross, foreshadowed here in Eden, that Jesus was going to come and destroy him.

Year after year Satan strives to pollute the world to keep Jesus from coming. Then he discovers that it is through the Jewish race that the Savior is going to come. Yes, the Messiah himself will be an Israelite. Over and over again he attacks the Jews. He does everything that he can to keep the Jews dispersed and destroyed. And yet God protects them for they are his own chosen people. One day he discovered that he has failed and Jesus is about to be born. Even now he is in the body of his mother Mary, his great entrance upon the scene of time is at hand. Desperately he runs ahead of him and does his best to see that the Savior is not born. Now, remember that Satan always has human instrumentalities through which he can do his work. And so through Herod, he sends out a decree that this year all of the world will be taxed in one place. It will be faster and money will be saved. So, the Lord Jesus in the body of his mother on the back of a donkey is jostled up and down over sixty miles of cobblestone streets and rough mountain roads, on the journey to Bethlehem. By every rule in the book, he should have been born dead or crippled. When he arrives at Bethlehem, Satan again has gone ahead of him and seen to it that there is a big convention in town and that all of the hotels are full. There is no place for the Savior to be born. He must be born in a manger!

It was not a beautiful hay pile as we depict it today. It was in the filth and the dung, and refuse of a cave in the side of a mountain that the master was born. Sickness and injury, disease, and death. All were a likely probability. Satan was doing his best. But Jesus was born alive and healthy. The reason? He had a good doctor. His name was the Holy Spirit. And what he has forgotten about medicine, modern doctors have never learned!

The Messiah is born and Satan is frantic. He does his

best to destroy Jesus Christ. He gets the Jews to disbelieve. He gets Barabbas to go free while Christ is condemned. He gets Pilate and Herod to say three times I find no fault in this man, nevertheless, let him be crucified.

He enters the heart of wicked men and they come to Him to crucify Him. Satan thinks that he has won. There he is! The one that was going to destroy me. There he is on a cross! Jesus bows his head and gives up the ghost. And he is dead. I can imagine that for the next three days as the body of Jesus lay in the tomb, Satan must have thrown the biggest drunk, the wildest celebration the world has ever seen.

But Sunday morning as the sun arose in the east, Satan rubbed his bleary eyes and looked across the valley and awoke to a strange new day. The bowels of the earth began to rumble. The tomb stone is rolled away and Jesus Christ comes forth. He comes out of the grave. He says "I have been into death, I've been into sin, I've been into hell, I've been into the grave. I am the resurrection and the light, he that believeth in me, though he were dead, yet shall he live. And the Savior wins and Satan has lost. Satan had failed to reckon with the resurrection!

He knows that his days are numbered and he knows that Jesus Christ is going to destroy him and bind him hand and foot and cast him into the lake of fire.

Now, he will attack man. For he says in his heart, "If I'm going to go to hell, I'm going to break the heart of God who loves man, by taking as many to hell with me as I can." And he comes to the sinner and points out the failures of the church. He says, "Look at the hypo-crites. Look at this, look at that, you haven't got the feeling, don't get excited, don't do it tonight, tomorrow, tomorrow." He comes with a hundred excuses. He seems to get some kind of neurotic, perverted, sense of satis-faction, by dragging everyone to hell with him.

But once in awhile someone is saved. They will say, "Get thee behind me, Satan." They will come to Christ and be converted. But do you think Satan leaves them alone? Not a chance! He says, "All right, I didn't get your soul, I'm going to get your influence. Don't get excited. Don't tithe; don't read the Bible, don't witness; don't go to church; go on just like you have been. After all, nobody likes a fanatic. You don't have to be peculiar. You don't want them to think that you are a religious nut. Don't get excited about living for Jesus Christ. Slow down, simmer down. Take it easy."

Satan is a master deceiver. The very word "Lucifer" means "Light bearer," or "One Who Shines." Don't think for one minute that Satan is as he is pictured: as a product of Greek mythology with a red suit and tail and pitch fork. No! He comes transformed as an angel of light. He shows you the man of distinction today, but he doesn't show you the man of extinction tomorrow. He shows you the socially elite business man today with Scotch on the rocks, but he doesn't show you the drunken bum laying in his own vomit in the gutter! He shows you the beautiful temptation of the forbidden fruit. He shows you the gorgeous seductive, wiles of a beautiful woman. But he doesn't show you that home broken in divorce and shame tomorrow. Satan is a liar!

He is a deceiver. Remember this. Satan has one plan.
He wants to destroy God. He wants to rise above God,
but he can't. So he is going to hurt the heart of God by
trying to attack God through God's people. He is the
arch enemy of our soul. He is the master deceiver.

Fourth, *consider the destruction of the devil.* What's
going to happen in the future. The Bible says he is
going to be banished for a thousand years, while there
is peace on earth. Then he will be loosed for a little
season, then cast into hell to deceive the nations no
more. Satan's days are numbered. And if you follow
him, so are yours. God has made you a free moral agent.
You do not have to follow God, and you do not have to
follow the devil. You can do what you want to do. But
what God does is merely to abide by your decision. If
you follow the devil now, all you will do is follow him
into hell. But if you follow Jesus in this life, then you
can follow him into the next life.

Fifth, *consider the Christian's defense against the
devil.* Don't laugh about the devil, don't tell jokes about
the devil, don't make jest about the devil. He's no
laughing matter. He is fierce, he is subtle, and he has
the power to destroy, to kill. He hates you, he hates me,
he hates the church, he hates righteousness, he hates
mothers, he hates the law, he hates God, he hates the
Bible and everything it stands for. Now, because his
days are numbered, he is ripping off the mask of his
disguise. He is becoming more open, more brazen than
he has ever been. He just has a little time. Sin is going
to become more obvious, nudity will become more
prevalent, temptation will be every where. In the last

days it's going to be worse than you and I ever thought possible. And unless you have a great defense against the devil, you do not have a chance of making a success out of the Christian life. You're as good as gone, you're a dead duck, you're lost, you've had it, you're finished. Unless in Jesus Christ you find your defense against the devil.

Listen to what the Bible says in Ephesians 6:10-17, "Finally, my brethren, be strong in the Lord, and in the power of his might. Put on the whole armour of God, that ye may be able to stand against the wiles of the devil. For we wrestle not against flesh and blood, but against principalities, against powers, against the rulers of the darkness of this world, against spiritual wickedness in high places. Wherefore take unto you the whole armour of God, that ye may be able to withstand in the evil day, and having done all, to stand. Stand therefore, having your loins girt about with truth, and having on the breastplate of righteousness; And your feet shod with the preparation of the gospel of peace; Above all, taking the shield of faith, wherewith ye shall be able to quench all the fiery darts of the wicked. And take the helmet of salvation, and the sword of the Spirit, which is the word of God."

This is your only defense. The helmet of salvation, the sword of the spirit, the word of God. The Bible says they overcame him by the blood of the Lamb.

Unless you have been saved by the blood of Jesus Christ, you will be overcome by the devil. Accept him today as your savior. You can win the game of life. You can defeat his majesty, the devil!

6
The Anatomy of a Murder

I call my sermon, "The Anatomy of a Murder," for I want us to dissect and analyze the downfall of one of the greatest men that ever lived. Here in the life of David is recorded one of the strangest combinations of two types of personalities in the Word of God. It is said of David that he is a man after God's own heart. No greater compliment was ever paid a man than that, that he was after the very heart of God. And yet David became a murderer. In the context of our modern society, there is no greater crime that a man can commit than to take the life of another human being. And yet, the Bible says that David, God's man, became a murderer.

What a complex and unique mingling of characteristics. On the one hand a man of greatness, a man after God's own heart, and on the other, a murderer. How did he go wrong? Let's look at God's man and see what happened in "The Anatomy of a Murder."

In act one we see the successes of David. When David was but a boy, the Philistine armies were oppressing Israel. None would fight their mighty giant Goliath. None that is, but David. Someone asked why he took five pebbles for his slingshot? Why not just one? He was a good shot! Because Goliath had four brothers and David was ready to fight them too. Before he went, they gave him armor of a sword, spear, and shield, but David could not walk with them. He had not tried them. Then David said, I come to you, Goliath, in the name of Jehovah, God of Israel. And all the enemies of God laughed. "Do you Israelites send a boy out to fight against a man like men?" And without a word, David took out the slingshot and twirled and flung a stone and hit giant Goliath in the temple. In a flash, he fell down and hit his head on a rock. David put his foot on his chest, and cut off his head, and it rolled down the hill and hit another rock. That was the world's first rock and roll.

David went into battle as a man but he came home a giant for God. Women and children lined the streets and cried, "Saul hath slain his thousands, and David his ten thousands" (1 Sam. 18:7). David was the national hero. You remember how David was chosen by the prophet Samuel, from the house of Jesse. The prophet looked at the first boy, then the second boy, the third, all the way to the seventh. "Do you not have another boy," they asked. "Is there one other that God would choose to be king over all Israel?" David's father said, "Well, there's but one other lad, the shepherd boy, David. But you wouldn't want him." "Bring him from the field," cried the prophet. They brought David in and God spoke to the heart of the prophet and said, "Here, this is the man." And David was chosen to be the future king at the youngest age of any man in all of Israel. Then at age thirty, he was annointed King.

David, God's brilliant man, God's handsome man, God's spiritual man. At thirty he was at the zenith of his career, and Satan set the trap, and baited it with beautiful Bathsheba.

And the curtain falls and rises again on act two, in the panorama of "The Anatomy of a Murder," the sins of David.

One day as David was walking on his rooftop, he looked down to see the woman bathing. I want you to remember that word down. Every step that a man takes away from God is a step down. The Bible says that the disciples went down from Jesus. Samson went down to Timnah, Jonah went down to get a ship going to Tarshish. When you look down, you go away from God, and when you go away from God you go down. David looked down.

It was noon. David should have been praying for at morning, noon, and night, the king always prayed. But this was one day that David forgot to pray and got into trouble. As he was walking, he looked, he lusted, and he stopped. Slowly, he rolled as a sweet morsel beneath the tongue, the taste of the forbidden fruit. The thought was planted. Satan had done his work. And the thought grew and grew until David was to commit the sin of adultery.

Young people, you give the devil an inch and he will take a mile. You give him a second and he'll take a lifetime. Give him a word and he will write a book. Give him a thought and he'll make a personality.

I know that it is out of context, but I think that we are well within the mark of solid scriptural application when we look at David's sins in the light of Psalm 1:1. Listen, "Blessed is the man that walketh not in the counsel of the ungodly, nor standeth in the way of sinners, nor sitteth in the seat of the scornful." Look at those words, walk, stand, and sit. What a picture it is of a man walking through life. Is it any accident that this is David's first psalm? As you walk through life you are going to have temptations, but the connecting link between walking and sitting, between temptation and participation is the second step, hesitation!! David should have turned his head as a Christian gentleman, and said, "God, forgive me. Get that picture out of my mind," and kept on walking. He never intended to sin, he never intended to participate. But he did, because he didn't keep walking. He didn't turn his head. He didn't go on. He stopped. And the minute you stop, the minute you consider sin, the minute you hesitate, the connecting link of hesitation between temptation and participation will be the one that will destroy you every time.

"As man thinketh in his heart, so is he." All of human personality gravitates toward the accomplishment of those things we think about. When David stopped, looked, and thought, he was a goner. You read that dirty book, go to that dirty show, listen to that dirty story, then you think about it!! Go your way, and try to forget it. But unless you get it out of your mind by the blood of Christ, as long as you hesitate and give consideration to it, the devil is getting it down in your blood, down in your veins, down in your heart, down in the core of your being, down in your innermost being. Eventually, it's going to get you. As a man think-eth in his heart, so is he!

The Bible says David sent for the woman and committed adultery with her. It was not long till she gave him the news, "I am with child." And God's man began to lie, to try to cover up the sin of adultery. Then he had to commit murder to cover that. He called for his commander and said, "The woman's husband, Uriah, the Hittite, is to be sent to the hottest battle front that he might be killed and I may have his wife."

David lusted, then he committed adultery, then he lied, then he committed murder. He had to commit one sin to cover up another. Sin after sin, temptation after temptation, failure after failure, he was caught in the quagmire of sin and went down. Down, down, farther, and farther away from God. Now he had killed a man. David, God's man. God's favorite. A man after God's own heart. With all the looks, the talent, the potential, of a brilliant life, but he had forfeited it all, for a mess of pottage.

And the curtain falls and rises again on act three, in the panorama of "The Anatomy of a Murder," the suffering of David. The Bible doesn't say, "Be sure your sins will be found out," but, "Be sure your sin will find you out" (Num. 32:23). No one may ever know, but you will know. Those things we plant come up in the lives of our children, friends, home, and future. No one may know, but you know. David knew! God knew. And someone else knew!

There was a faithful prophet in the land that knew what had happened. Thank God for preachers who are not afraid to tell the truth. One day Nathan the prophet came and told David the story.

"One day a traveler came through town, and a rich family wanted to entertain him. But rather than slaying one of their own sheep for the banquet, they stole the one little ewe lamb of one of their poor neighbors. David said, "That man must pay fourfold." The prophet of God pointed at David, and said, "Thou art the man" (2 Sam. 12:7). He was speaking of David. The stranger of lust had come through town. David wanted to entertain him. David had everything. But he broke up the home and stole the wife of one of his men. He took the one little ewe lamb, he took the one priceless and precious possession from the breast of that man that loved her with all of his heart.

David smote his breast and cried, "I have sinned. God, forgive me." And the prophet said, "David your sins are forgiven. But the sword shall never depart out of the house of David." And it never did.

Remember David, you planted your wild oats. Now, you are going to reap the harvest. You've sown to the wind, now reap the whirlwind. Remember too, David, you said, "Fourfold." "Whatsoever a man soweth, that shall he also reap" (Gal. 6:7). Not only do we reap what we sow, but we reap later than we sow, and we reap more than we sow. David, you're going to reap more than you've sown—fourfold.

Bathsheba gave birth to a beautiful baby boy. David had his heart set on that little son, but on his eighth day, God called him home. "David, the baby is dead! Now, the first harvest is in the barn. But you said fourfold, David. Hear his words as he prays, "Oh, would to God I had never sinned. Would to God I would never looked. Would to God I had never have hesitated." But he had, and now he would pay.

David had a beautiful daughter named Tamar. Amnon, David's wicked son, ravished and raped his own sister. The courier brings the news. "David, your daughter has been attacked by the hand of your own son." Now, the second harvest is in the barn. Whatsoever a man soweth that shall he also reap. But you said, fourfold.

Absalom, David's other son, hearing what has happened comes against Amnon and kills his own brother. Again the courier comes riding, riding, through the night, "David! David! Get the king! Bring King David!" David, now the third harvest is in the barn. "Amnon, your son, whom you loved is dead. Slain at the hand of Absalom, his own brother."

See him as again and again, night after night, he paces back and forth across the rooftop. That very spot from whence he first looked. "Oh, God, would that I had never stopped. Would to God I had never looked. Would to God that I'd never committed that sin." But David, you said fourfold and there is one more harvest to reap. Night after night he waits. Night after night he prays, "Oh, God, what now? Is the sword never to depart from the house of David?"

The Bible tells us that David's son Absalom raises the standard of revolt against him. Riding through the night Absalom is snatched from the back of his horse as his hair is caught in the forks of a giant oak tree.

David's own soldiers, never dreaming he would not want them to kill his own rebellious son, fill his body with poisonous darts, and Absalom is dead. Again the courier comes riding, riding, riding through the night. "Get the king, open the gate. More bad news, David." David steps to his rooftop and his heart races with the wind. "Now, what is it? Oh, God, what is going to happen next?" "David, Absalom, your son, is dead." And with all the pathos, and agony the heart of man has ever known, David falls on his knees, right there on that very spot from which he had looked at Bathsheba, and cries with bitter tears, "Oh, Absalom, Absalom, my son, would to God that I had died in thy stead."

And the curtain falls on the third act in the panorama of a murder, the awful consequences, the inevitable suffering of David.

Now, listen to the surrender of David. Thank God, he is a God of mercy. David writes the fifty-first psalm, that psalm that many a man has claimed, because the gospel we preach is the gospel of good news. A gospel for broken men. The gospel of beginning again. The gospel of the second chance. See him as he rises from his place, washes his face, goes to his couch, and begins to pray: "Have mercy upon me, O God, according to thy lovingkindness: according to the multitude of thy tender mercies blot out my transgressions. Wash me throughly from mine iniquity, and cleanse me from my sin. For I acknowledge my transgressions: and my sin is ever before me. Against thee, thee only, have I sinned, and done this evil in thy sight: That thou mightest be justified when thou speakest, and be clear when thou judgest. Behold, I was shappen in iniquity, and in sin did my mother conceive me. Behold, thou desirest truth in the inward parts: and in the hidden part thou shalt make me to know wisdom. Purge me with hyssop, and I shall be clean: wash me, and I shall be whiter than snow. Make me to hear joy and gladness; that the bones which thou hast broken may rejoice. Hide thy face from my sins, and blot out all mine iniquities. Create in me a clean heart, O God; and renew a right spirit within me. Cast me not away from thy presence; and take not thy holy spirit from me. Restore unto me the joy of thy salvation; and uphold me with thy free spirit. Then will I teach transgressors thy ways; and sinners shall be converted unto thee."

Listen to David, God's man, begging for mercy. "Wash me throughly from within." That second verse is not thoroughly, it is THROUGHLY. He was dirty on the inside. He wanted to be cleansed on the inside. "Against thee and thee only have I sinned." But he hadn't. He had sinned against the woman. He had sinned against her husband. He had sinned against God. He had sinned against his children. He had sinned against his influence. And he sinned against the kingdom of God. David prays and prays. "Make these broken bones to rejoice. Hide your face from my sins. Create in me a clean heart, O God." He felt dirty within. "Give me a clean spirit." "Oh, God, don't take your Holy Spirit from me. Keep on using me I pray thee. Without thee, I can do nothing." He doesn't say save me again. He doesn't say "restore unto me my salvation." He says, "Restore unto me the joy of thy salvation."

The curtain falls and David is forgiven. But I don't think that things were ever the same again. He was never quite as happy. He was never quite as usable. He was never quite as complete as he was before. The sword never departed from the house of David.

Years ago in Ohio a teen-age boy came home drunk one night from the senior prom. He begged his dear mother's forgiveness, but it happened again and again. By the time he was twenty-three, to make a long story short, he was the town drunk. He had been divorced three times. Night after night his parents who loved him, sobered him up, and put him to bed. Over and over again he promised it would never happen again. But somehow it always did.

One night he was gloriously saved. His mother took him to the bedroom to show him the closet door. "Son," she said, "The first night you came home drunk years ago, I painted a big red heart on the inside of this door. Every night you've come home drunk, every night you've done wrong, I've driven a nail in the heart, just as you have driven a nail in my heart. Look at it." Dramatically, flinging the door open, she showed the boy the heart filled with nails. He fell on his knees and was saved. Time went by and he went back to his last wife. He joined the church and did well. A year later he was at his mother's home again. Somehow he seemed to be restless. "Mother," he said, "Let's go upstairs again. I want to see that door one more time. For you see the memory of those nails, is driving me crazy. She said, "All right son, every time you go to church, every time you do good for Christ, I'll pull one of those nails out of the door. Now, that you have been saved, we'll record the good deeds of your life." Somehow it seemed to please him for awhile. Soon all the nails were gone. The years had come and gone. The young man was now an old man. The mother lay dying. Holding her hand in his, he said, "Mother, you've loved me, you've been responsible for my being saved, you brought me to my senses. Now, I want to ask you to get rid of that door. I can't stand it any more." "Why son," the mother said, "What's the matter? The nails, look, they are gone, they are all gone. Thank God, they are all gone." "Ah, yes," said the boy, "The nails are gone, but the holes are still there!!!"

You can go out into the garage and take an ax and sharpen it and cut off your hand. God will forgive you, but you still won't have a hand. You kill a man and God will forgive you as he did David, but the man will still be dead. You can pull out the nails, but the holes will still be there.

My plea to you is this: Don't drive in any more nails.

7
The Sexual Revolution

May I qualify myself to you. I led a dance band professionally for four and one half years. I have preached over 500 revival meetings, to close to a million teen-agers, through the years, and then for the last five years have been pastor of a church that happens to be one of the youngest in America. We have about six hundred students in junior high, high school, and college who attend our church every Sunday morning. They sit at the front and take up the entire front half of the church. About 200 of them are from colleges. We have great numbers of high-school teen-agers as well. And we are fortunate in that the football captains, beauty queens, and student-body leaders, and so forth are all in our church. We have students from thirteen high schools. Every year we are able to get the football stadium for a revival because the school board says that they realize there is a tangible difference in the schools of our city because of the impression and the impact of these students. I average baptizing nearly four college or high school students every Sunday. That's nearly 200 a year, and I haven't won a teen-ager to Christ in five years. I don't have to. My kids do it. And I'm proud of them.

The average age is twenty years, seven months, and so I spend up to twenty hours a week doing marital counseling, talking to people about marital problems.

So, when I talk about a sexual revolution, I'm not telling you something that I've read out of a book. Under the guise of the new morality, we are experiencing a revolution in moral standards. The watchword is freedom.

Sometime ago in a large article, I read the story of the following remarks about morals. It said something like this:

"It is a shame the way modern students carry on. They act and walk and dress in manners obviously intended to entice sexual appetites. Coeds engage in all kinds of wild orgies and drunkenness. Cheating on examinations is considered normal and acceptable. Surely we are experiencing the decline of the moral structure of the universe and the decay of modern life."

These words, or a paraphrase of them, were written by Aristophanes, the Greek dramatist five hundred years before the birth of Jesus Christ. It's not a new morality at all. It's the same old immorality we've always had. But although their motto is freedom, they don't really know what freedom is. And they have, as Abraham Lincoln said of the liquor traffic, the answer to everything and the solution to nothing.

Anson Mount, *Playboy*'s representative to the college campus, was asked this question by a student: "Mr. Mount, for five years I have read *Playboy*, I've dressed *Playboy*, I've lived *Playboy*, I've been a real *Playboy* cat. But now I've got a question. I want to know what is the

Playboy cat supposed to do when his kitty's going to have kittens?" Mr. Mount's sick reply was, "I'm afraid we don't have the answer to everything. You'll have to see an obstetrician about that one."

They asked Hugh Heffner in *Life* magazine if he with his Methodist background intended after all was said and done that his daughter then approaching sixteen would live by his philosophy. Mr. Heffner said, "I would rather not be pinned down, I would rather not have to answer that question."

The answer to everything, but the solution to nothing. And their quick snapshot answer is always freedom. Freedom, freedom, down with Victorian morality and the Ten Commandments. We are free after all! A good time is the purpose for life and man is the master of his own fate. That kind of philosophy caused the Russians to lay down their Bibles, pick up their guns, and start the Bolshevik revolution. It caused eight million Jews to be burned in Germany under Nazism, and has created a moral atmosphere in which marriage is little more than a social convenience. And they don't understand that the Commandments of God, the restraints placed upon human nature and the teachings of Jesus Christ in the New Testament are not because God is against us, but because he is for us. God wants us to be happy. He wants us to be free. But they don't understand what freedom is.

I believe that the sorriest advertisement for Christianity is an old sourpuss look. The philosophy of religion that is being sold to young people today is kind of like the little boy who was playing in the garage. His mother heard him, and looked out the window and said, "Tommy, I don't care what you are doing, whatever it is, stop it!" Now, there are those who think that's what religion is all about. That God is a mean old man who doesn't want us to have any fun, and he goes around beating our brains out everytime we start to have a good time.

As a woman said, "It seems that everything that is any fun is either fattening or sinful." Well, such is not the case. And so the new morality crowd comes along and says they're going to free us. Let's kick over the traces, let's burn up the Bible, let's destroy the Commandments, let's set up our own rules. Again the watchword is freedom. Freedom, freedom, freedom; we're all going to be free.

You know what? I like that! I buy that! I really do! I agree with that philosophy ten thousand percent. And I remind you that the greatest person that ever lived, came from heaven, and said, "I have come that ye might have freedom. I am the truth, and the truth shall make you free." Yes, God wants you to be free. But what I'm saying to you is that the greatest hoax that has been perpetrated on a generation of young people in all of history is the bill of goods you're getting today as to what freedom really is!!

A girl came home from school the other day with a big sign that said, "Down with conformity." Her mother said, "You get rid of that, right this minute." The girl started crying, and said, "But Mama everybody's got one."

Freedom, freedom! We all want to be free. But I'm

afraid we don't know what freedom is. Listen. Everything that I want to say to you is based upon this simple premise. Freedom is good. Freedom is to be desired. Freedom should be the drive, the desire, the purpose, the thrust, and the crux of every philosophy of life. That's what living is all about. That's the purpose of religion. That's why Jesus came. That's the teaching of the New Testament.

But, Satan is selling you a bill of goods about what freedom is. Freedom is not merely the right to rebel. Freedom comes by way of discipline. Without discipline you don't have any freedom. Let's take a few examples. Take the matter of smoking. It gives us a sense of security, kind of like the old pacifier. A lot of big babies go around today with two-inch pacifiers in their mouths. It gives them a sense of security. A sense of fulfilment. Really makes them feel like they're somebody. It will do strange things to your personality. And so teen-agers, start out to smoke as a status symbol, as a new vehicle of their maturity and their rebellion against their parents, to grow up fast, to be somebody. That little two-inch cigarette has become the vehicle of their freedom and an expression of their independence.

Now, I want you to see them when they're forty-five or fifty years old. They'd like to quit, but they can't. They're a slave to it, and it's affected their whole life.

Here's a young person who has the courage to dare to be different. He says I don't think it's smart to smoke and I don't do it. Now, he's free to sleep at night. He's free to enjoy his food, he's free to live 10 percent longer. Now who's free and now who's a slave?

Freedom isn't the right to do what you get good and ready to do. Real freedom comes by discipline. Unless you pay the price, you're not going to be free at all.

The same thing is true of drinking. A student begins to drink. It becomes a vehicle of his maturity. Why he is a cocky somebody. Oh, it does him good to buy a six pack in front of a girl, to have a few bottles over at the fraternity. It makes him somebody, he grows up. Now, I want you to see that same fellow when he's fifty years old. He's become an alcoholic. He's a drunken bum in the streets. He's lost his home, his job, he's lost his fortune, he's lost his health, he's lost his self-respect. He's a slave to that bottle. Now, here's college student B over here. He played by the rules. They laughed at him. They called him a fanatic. They called him religious, they called him square. But he had better sense than to let that bother him. Now, he's got a good body, a good job, self-respect, and all of the things that go with it. Now, he's free to make money. He's free to have a good job. He can take a vacation, buy a new television and send his kids to college. He's free to do what he wants to do. Now who's free? Freedom is not the right to rebel—freedom comes by discipline. No discipline—no freedom.

Here's a student who says, "Nobody is going to make me study." Some little fourteen-year-old hot rodder with sideburns half way down to his ankles, dark leather jacket, and a motorcycle. Man, he's somebody. No square teacher is going to make him study a bunch of history and English.

Now he's eighteen years old, he's flunked out of

school. He's got his girl friend pregnant, he's living in a two-bit shack making forty bucks a week, pumping gas or pushing a broom. He's a slave to his own ignorance. He'll never go anywhere.

But here's a student who paid the price. He stayed in school and made the grades. Now, he's got the job. He's got the leadership. He's got everything. He's something! But the dropout back there is a slave to his own ignorance.

God doesn't tell you to do some things and not to do some things just to make life miserable for you. He wants you to be free. He wants you to live. But you are being sold a bill of goods as to what freedom really is.

You say I'll drive which ever way I want to drive on the highway. Nobody is going to make me stop at a red stoplight. I'm free. I'll go where I want. I'll do what I want to do. No matter what the signs say, no matter what the speed limit is. I'm free.

All right, go ahead. You kill each other. You tear up your car. Everybody's dead. Now, what kind of freedom do you have? You're not free to get home unless you play by the rules of the road. Unless somebody disciplines themselves, unless somebody plays by the rules, unless somebody pays the price in Vietnam, and Germany, and Japan, and everywhere, then you're not free to sit in this service and talk about it. Freedom comes by discipline. Unless you discipline yourself and pay the price, you don't have any freedom.

And it's the same way with sex. Sex is God's good and beautiful gift to the world. And sex saved and used in

Christian marriage as God planned will be a life-giving force and a strength that will drive you to the top in life. Listen! You cannot separate the sex act from the total blending of two personalities that God intended that it be and expect to have anything. Sex demands security for the woman. The very nature of the sex act demands that the man meet all of her needs. It says, I'm paying our bills, I'm taking care of the children, I'm providing your defense. I'm making you secure. Sex for the man demands responsibility. It demands obligation. Unless he is able to do these things, unless he becomes the defender of her life, her chastity, her ego, her needs, her children, her future, her everything, then it has become a frustrating experience for him.

Sex demands confession for both. When two people love each other, they want to walk side by side. They want to walk hand in hand. They want the world to know. But young people, listen to me!! Outside the bonds of matrimony, you don't have contentment. You don't have security. You don't have publicity. You don't have responsibility. You don't have all that it is suppose to express. You only have an isolated part of its entirety. And you cannot end up with anything but frustration, confusion, problems, and conflicts.

Recently, I have been dealing with two couples. One couple has been married seventeen years and one twenty-four years. In each case they had sexual experience one time before they were married. But now for years, the haunting question has come to their minds, that has almost driven them to insanity. I could never trust you before with me, how can I be dead sure I can trust you with someone else? In neither case is any of the four being unfaithful to each other. But they suspect that they are, because the respect and trust that must be brought into a marriage is not there. Now, they are not free, they are slaves to the past. Immediately, the bloodhounds of guilt and confusion, the fear of discovery, are all set loose. And many a young person is going to carry to the grave an ego, a personality warped, marred, twisted, because of one experience outside of marriage. Because of one experience before marriage. One experience has eaten away the vital foundation of trust and respect that must be in marriage. There must be security. There must be confidence. There must be confession. There must be trust. There must be respect. There must be responsibility.

It is as frustrating as playing a piano with only one string. The sexual relationship is only a part of the total blending of two personalities becoming one. And sex outside of Christian marriage is but an isolated part of the entirety that only leads to frustration.

Oh, but I wish you could see the young couples in our church that have played by the rules, that disciplined themselves and reaped the rewards. Sure it's tough. And it will get tougher. Cheer up, it's going to get worse. The temptation, the problems, and the looseness will become much, much more appealing.

But those who are free to live, to possess, to develop, to have, are those who realize God knew what he was talking about; and the limitations that he placed on their morals were for their good. So, that they might be free indeed.

Billy Graham has given us some concrete suggestions for young persons who want to find real freedom in life.

Number one. Watch your eyes. The eyes are the gateway to the heart. Through the eyes enter most of the things that cause us problems. Job said, "I have made a covenant with mine eyes; why then should I think upon a maid?" (Job 31:1). Now, you say old Job must have had a time, going around stumbling in the dark with his eyes shut. But wait. There are looks and then there are looks. You can't avoid the first look, but you can avoid the second look. David, who ought to know more about it than anybody said, "Blessed is the man that walketh not in the counsel of the ungodly, nor standeth in the way of sinners, nor sitteth in the seat of the scournful" (Ps. 1:1).

If you are going to have some positive approaches to life, you're going to have to begin by learning to control your eyes. Because what we think about, we tend to become. You say, "Well, preacher, you can't help looking sometimes." No, you can't help the birds from flying over your head, but you can keep them from building nests in your hair. Watch your eyes!

Secondly, watch your mind. Don't let wrong thoughts stay in it for a long time. As a man thinketh in his heart, so is he.

Third, watch your lips. Out of the abundance of the heart, the lips speak. What John tells me about Bill tells me more about John than it tells me about Bill. Don't tell dirty, off-color stories and don't laugh at those that are foolish enough to tell them. You will be amazed how your silence, your refusal to laugh will cut down the individual who is painting the air blue with obscenities. Don't identify yourself with that kind of ignorance. Watch your lips.

Fourth, watch what you read. The newsstands are filled with filth. You ought to avoid it like the plague.

Fifth, watch your dress. Be very careful about that. Now, I'm not talking to men, I'm talking to women. There's nothing very appealing about a man's boney, hairy legs. But it doesn't work that way with members of the opposite sex. God has not made the body of the male particularly attractive.

Recently a very beautiful girl said, "Before I was a Christian frankly I used to dress to knock the daylights out of the men. But now that I am a Christian I dress everywhere I go as if Jesus Christ were going to be my escort."

You young women say what is in good taste? What is modest? How should I dress? You dress as though Jesus were your escort. Then you won't go very far wrong. As women go, the men go. Wouldn't it be wonderful if the girls of America would start a new trend next year? A trend of modesty? You can do it! The woman is the glory of God. Her beauty is the glory of God's beauty. Young women, one bad seductive female can do more harm than a hundred bad men. But one beautiful, sharp, Christian gal can do more good than a hundred boys can do. Set the pace. Be a beauty queen for Jesus!!

Sixth, watch your amusements. Now, these are just cornball things that you've heard all your life but that we need to be reminded of time and time again. I think that you should be rather selective in the movies that you see. And while I'm at it, and you can agree or disagree, I want to tell you that after five years of leading a dance band, and after seventeen years of working very closely with teen-agers, I believe the dance is one of the quickest ways to get yourself in trouble.

Seventh, avoid the wrong company. Now, girls, some of you and your boy friends are already going too far, you're already too close. And if that boy doesn't respect you enough to keep his hands off of you, then get a new one! Love seeketh not its own. If he really loves you he will respect you.

The freedom that this day has given young people, has brought us to the position that outside of actually living as man and wife together, there are few intimacies and conveniences that the modern teen-age couple does not enjoy. And for far too many the temptation is just too much. So, if you're getting yourself in trouble, get out of that tempting situation fast.

Eighth, read and memorize some Scripture every day. The Word of God will give you power to resist Satan.

Last, make sure Jesus Christ is in your heart. I want the best for you. God wants the best for you. But you have to play by the rules. So, make sure he's in your heart and life, or you can't make it. Go out to win in the rebellious war of the sexual revolution. Be one of the good guys. Wear a white hat. Dare to be different. Don't say, "Man, everybody's doing it." I guess that will be the theme song of hell. "Everybody's doing it." Any old dead fish can float down the stream. Anybody can be one of the crowd, one of the little boxes all in a row, one of the little paper doll cutouts. You see one today, you've seen them all. They all dress alike, they all talk alike, they all look alike, they all smell alike. Dare to be different. Go upstream. Any dead fish can go to hell. Get a backbone with more in it than a wet noddle. Suppose they call you a fanatic? It's your life, your conscience, and your future!! And one day when they are crying, you'll be laughing. One day when they have had it, when they have blown all of their fuses and busted all their gaskets and popped all their corks, you'll just be starting to live. Make sure he's in your heart and life or you stand very little chance of winning the game of life.

8
This I Believe

For me to tell you everything that I believe would take a long time. For me to tell you everything that I am sure of would not take nearly so long. But I do want to crystalize in your minds some of the eternal truths that we as Christians hold dear. I am impressed that in any church on Sunday morning there are many folks who have probably picked up just enough little tidbits of information along the way to be thoroughly confused. Sort of like the fellow who went off to a convention with a little sign stuck on him, "IAK." Someone came up and said, "What does that mean?" He answered, "That means I am confused." He said, "Man, you don't spell confused with a 'K.'" The fellow said, "You don't know how confused I am."

Let us remind ourselves again of some important things we should remember that God has used to bless us to make us what we are through the years.

First of all I believe in being saved. I want you to remember that word. You are going to hear it less and less in years to come. We have the idea that we have to become very relevant. We have the idea that we have to change our methods and change our message. But I have found out that it is not our responsibility to make the gospel relevant. It is our responsibility to preach it, and it is the work of the Holy Spirit to make it relevant.

They say in these days that the old words will not do. Men do not die any more, they merely pass away. They slip off, they go to that great revival in the sky. Folks are not lost anymore, they are merely unreached, uninvolved, unenlisted, or unchurched. Men are not sinners anymore. They merely suffer from a temporary evolutionary lag, or an extreme neurosis, or from a downward stumble on an upward path. But to say that men sin is hush-hush and taboo. The modern world in which we live does not believe that men sin.

And this word *saved* is a word that we are getting farther and farther away from, too. I know that it may seem a very small thing, but I believe that it is a sign of a trend in the wrong direction away from those things that are the most important in all of life: that men have a tangible, literal, knowable, experience with God. I have found that very seldom can I get the average church member to even use the word *saved*. I asked them about their conversion. "Oh," they say, "I went up when I was fifteen. Or I joined when I was eleven. Or I went in when I was thirteen. My husband and I made our decisions at a certain age."

They are not saved anymore. They just come for baptism, they come for profession, they come for church membership. They do everything but get saved. We stand up and glibly say, "Who'll come by profession," and who will come by letter." And the average man in the pew doesn't know profession from possession, or letter from better. I believe we need to remind ourselves that men are lost and that if you are going to go to heaven, you must have a definite experience with God, something that is knowable, something that is called being saved.

When did we get away from getting down on our knees? When did men get away from praying to God? What's wrong with a man talking to God until he knows that the power of God is come into his life and he has had an experience with God? Much of the uncertainty, much of the confusion, much of the doubt and hesitation with which so many people approach the service of the Lord Jesus Christ is a result of a careless introduction into the kingdom of God.

Now, I know that you do not have to get down on your knees to be saved. You may not have to directly pray to God to be saved. You can say, "I believe, yes preacher, I am accepting Christ." You can only address the minister. I understand that. But I have found in my ministry that it is from those decisions in which we merely shake hands or sign a card or nod our head to some question that most of the doubts come. I believe in men getting down before God—that whosoever shall call upon the name of the Lord shall be saved. I believe in praying to God and asking Jesus to come into your heart and save your poor lost soul.

Before I was a Christian I thought religion was an intangible, superfluous nothing. But then I discovered something that changed my life. I didn't just come and sign a card, I didn't just go up or come for baptism, or make a profession. Something happened on the inside of my heart. I found a friend who is all to me, says the songwriter, and I have made a profession, made a profession, profession? No! I don't know about you but that just doesn't do much for me. I like it like this:

> "I've found a friend who is all to me, His love is ever true;
>> I love to tell how He lifted me And what his grace can do for you.
>> Saved by His power divine, Saved to new life sublime!
>> Life now is sweet, and my joy is complete, For I'm saved, saved, saved!

I believe that we need to keep foremost in our religion that the experience that changes men's lives, gets them ready to live and ready to die, puts the blood of Christ in the heart by faith, and makes men children of the living God and fit disciples for the kingdom of heaven is that they have been to Calvary. Their lives have been transformed and they have been saved!

Secondly, I believe in baptism for people who have been saved. Now, you say preacher, that is a relatively unimportant matter. It is not! I believe it to be the first step of faithfulness in the service of Jesus Christ. And may I say to you that I can number on one hand the people I have ever known who made success of their Christian life who did not follow Christ in baptism.

Now, we as Christians, obviously realize that there are some unique beliefs from the Word of God as to what constitutes New Testament baptism. Let me state them for you.

First of all, baptism is for someone who has been saved, not for someone who is lost. That's why, when someone is really converted, regardless of what they have done in the past, they are to be baptized.

I could go downtown if I were unmarried and buy a wedding ring from every store in town and pretend to be married. But it would be meaningless to try to say what this ring implies if I were not really married. Baptism is a sign, it is a symbol, like a wedding ring, that one is united in marriage. As Jesus was buried and rose for me, I am identifying myself with him. As this ring is unending, I am identifying myself with my wife and the unending nature of our relationship. Baptism evidences something; it means something. And if nothing has happened on the inside of your life when you were baptized, and you have really been saved since you were baptized, then your earlier baptism meant nothing. You need to be baptized properly, correctly, publicly, spiritually, having been saved.

Then baptism must be not only for the right person, but by the right authority. Who has the authority to baptize people? Only a creditable, New Testament church. That's why we say, "How many of you join in receiving this one?" And authorize the pastor who has no power to baptize except it be given to him each time by the church to do so.

Many believe that one can go about indiscriminately baptizing whomever they will. But, authority must always be given. "Can anyone forbid water seeing that these have received the Holy Ghost as well as we?" Baptism must be by the right authority.

And then it must be by the right method, immersion. The word "baptism" is from a Greek word, "baptiso," which literally means to bury or to cover up. It symbolizes the death of the old and the birth of the new. When Jesus Christ came into my heart, the old personality, the old nature, that rebellion and war against God died; and a new nature, a willing nature, the nature of the living Christ was implanted into my life. Ladies and gentlemen you are missing one of the most beautiful experiences and privileges and obligations of the Christian life if you have not yet followed Jesus Christ in baptism. As a man wears the ring of his wife or his lodge, as he puts on the wings of the Air Force or the symbol of that organization to which he belongs, so does baptism identify him with Jesus Christ.

Most scholars in the world will admit, regardless of his denomination, that New Testament baptism was by immersion. "We merely don't do it that way," they say, "for convenience sake." But, as Christians, we certainly should do it that way for Scripture's sake.

If I had a dog that died and I wanted to bury him, and the word "baptize" means to bury, I would not go out in a field and stretch him out on the ground and sprinkle some dirt on his head, and call him buried. I would dig a hole and put him in it and cover him up. Now, there are many of you who, since you have believed with saving faith on the name of Jesus Christ, have as yet not publicly come down the aisle on an invitation and said, "Count on me, I'm one of you, I want to be identified with Jesus." May I say to you that you will never in a thousand years find joy in consistent fidelity to Jesus Christ and in doing his will until you have first done this initial commandment of our Lord.

In the book of Acts, some people were baptized again, identifying themselves with the doctrinal position of the new group to which they adhered. When we change schools or organizations, it is not uncommon to wear the new badge of that organization. If a man's wife dies and he marries again, he will wear the ring of his new wife. Baptism at the hands of a certain church says that I understand the Word of God as do you. I agree with you. I am one with you.

If you are considering joining a particular church and you cannot understand completely why you are asked to be baptized, let me say this to you: Frankly, I would not mind to be baptized every Sunday. If I wanted to be a Baptist or a Methodist, I'd do what they asked. We take of the Lord's Supper more than once. I would not object to submitting to baptism again, because it preaches a beautiful sermon. We baptize every Sunday morning in our church because we have more people there then than at any other time. And in so doing, we present a beautiful picture of the death, burial, and resurrection of Jesus Christ. And you who would be baptized into the fellowship of this church, would without saying a word, preach a sermon on the life, death, and resurrection of Christ. Someone might see it and visualize Calvary and be saved.

Number three, I believe in the church. I believe in the local New Testament church. The word "church" is used two different ways in the Bible. About 10 percent of the time, it is referring to all who have been saved, as a great world church. And to be sure, that great world church is being formed. But it is not in reality complete yet and will not be until the last soul is saved before Jesus Christ comes. Until that time we are to identify ourselves and serve through local New Testament churches, bodies of believers in the Word of God as are we. Most of the New Testament references are to the local church.

To be sure, there are many wonderful organizations in this world. But ladies and gentlemen, Jesus Christ did not come and die, and bleed for, and establish the Masons, or the Moose, or the Odd Fellows, or the Elk, or the Youth for Christ, or the Girl Scouts, or the Red Cross. Christ came for the church. He died for the church. He established the church. He left the church. He is coming for the church. And it is through the program of the local New Testament churches that the task of missions and world evangelism and worship is to be accomplished. What a privilege to belong to a church like this, a great citadel of faith and evangelism across two nations and around this part of the United States.

Privilege neglected, privilege abused, becomes privilege lost. There are places in this world where it is not possible to give a public invitation. There are places in this world where it is not wise to have your name on the roll of a church for reasons of safety. There are places in this world where guards stand at the door and watch as decisions are made.

But I thank God that in this land, still one nation under God it is, you and I have the privilege of coming to a gospel-believing church on Sunday morning, hearing the choir sing, "Just as I am, without one plea, but that thy blood was shed for me," have the privilege of putting back our shoulders and walking down the aisle and saying: "I am one of you. Count on me. I'm a Christian, too." What a privilege to belong to a New Testament church. And have you used it yet? You brought your insurance, your job, your family, your furniture; have you brought your relationship to God through a local New Testament church to the city in which you live?

I believe in being saved, I believe in baptism for saved people, I believe in the church for those that are saved and baptized.

You know what I'm going to say last, don't you? I'll bet we could have a survey here, and three out of four would know my last point. I believe in Baptists. I really do. Now, in case you didn't catch that, that was B-A-P-T-I-S-T-S. I believe in Baptists. And in this day of ecumenicism, in which many people are so broad-minded they are flat headed, I want us to remind ourselves of some things that we are and that distinctly make us a unique denomination. I believe it is the greatest soul-winning denomination in the history of the world. Somebody said in 1954, when we had as our goal, "a million more in 54," "God help us if we get another million like the six million we already have." Somebody said Baptists are many, but they are not much. And to be sure there are numbers of groups that God is using and blessing. But let me share with you why I have chosen to keep my life and my ministry and my influence within the framework of this denomination.

I believe in Baptists because of their past. Now, you can say that Baptists started here or that they started there, but if you will check the encyclopedia, you will find the following expression under "B" for Baptists. "As to the origin of Baptists there can be no certain date." We cannot be traced by what we have been called but by what we have believed across the centuries.

I believe in Baptists because of the present. To be a Baptist means some things. It means that I believe in the infallibility and the final authority of the Word of God, for one thing. And we believe in the priesthood of the believer. Once there was a Catholic man and a Baptist man who worked at Tinker Air Base, in Oklahoma City. They were discussing their various ideas of religion. The Catholic said, "We confess our sins to the priest." The Baptist said: "Not us. We go straight to God." "Well," the Baptist said to the Catholic, "tell me, sir, does the priest ever sin?" "Oh, yes, no one's perfect." "Well, to whom would he confess his sins?" "That's easy," said the Catholic, "probably to the bishop." "Does he ever sin?" "I suppose so." "To whom does he confess his sin?" "Well, perhaps to one of the cardinals." "And sir, would he ever do wrong?" "Well, yes. I guess he would confess his sins to the pope." "And what of the pope, does he ever sin? Is he perfect?" "No, no one is perfect." "Well, to whom does the pope confess his sins?" "Well," the Catholic man said, "I guess he would confess his sins to God." "Oh, I see," said the Baptist, "The pope's a Baptist, too."

But we believe as Christians in the final, exclusive authority of the Word of God and that every man is his own priest before God through the blood of Jesus Christ. We also believe in separation of church and state, that salvation is by the grace of God apart and exclusive from works, and we believe in the autonomy of the local church. That's what makes Baptists, Baptists.

And I believe in something else. I believe in Baptists because of their future. Throughout the history of the world, you will discover that nearly every great denomination that once was, but no longer is, has gone down the drain on the wings of three pitfalls.

Number one: They became cold, dead, and formal in their service and thought they were worshiping when in reality they were dying. The Bible says love thy God with all thy mind, and all thy heart, and all thy soul. And unless the emotion of man, the heart of man, as well as the intellect, of man is stimulated and a man is thereby motivated to want to do what he intellectually knows to do, the demise of a denomination is not far behind.

Then another thing: Great denominations have gone down the drain because in their schools, in higher education, they have begun to disbelieve the Word of God. The Bible says, "Beware lest any man spoil you through philosophy" (Col. 2:8). Let us continue to be a people that just don't have any better sense than to believe the Bible as the Word of God.

Third, and last, I believe in the future of Baptists because in every great denomination that once was great but now is a crumbling shell of what it used to be, there has been the substitute of the second best for the first best. And men have had the idea that it was their job to make the world a better place in which to live. I don't believe Baptists will make that mistake. No. It is not the message and the mission of the New Testament church to make the world a better place to live. It is our calling to make better men to live in the world. Denominations that have turned to the hot butter of social reform, from the diamond-sharp cutting edge of evangelism to that degree, are fallen and decayed.

I believe that God has raised this giant denomination of ours as a mighty evangelic tool to win millions to Christ. And I pray that this church, the bulwark of power, the citadel of truth that it is, may continue to ever be at the forefront of evangelism and truth in the Word of God and preaching the Gospel and evangelizing the world. I believe we will stay on the right track!

I believe in being saved. Have you been saved? We believe that men ought to be baptized by immersion, identifying themselves with Christ after they have been saved. And have you been? I believe in the church, the local church. Do you? This city needs what you and God's people here together can do.

In London many years ago, a young boy moved to a new neighborhood. The lad was lost. Going to a bobby, a policeman, he asked him how to get home. He said, "Son, what is your name. You are a new boy, and I do not know you." But the boy had forgotten his name. "Well, Son, where do you live." He said, "Saint, Saint, something." The lad tried, but he couldn't remember. The policeman said, "Son, they are all named Saint something around this part of London." The little boy thought and said, "I do remember this. My new house is next to a church." The policeman said, "But Son, there are so many churches in this part of London." Dejected, the lad turned and started to walk away. He hadn't gone ten feet when he remembered. His little eyes lit up and he turned around and said, "Bobby, Bobby, I've got it." My house is next to a big church. And my church has a great big cross on top of it. Bobby, hold me up. Take me back to the cross, let me see the cross, and when I get back to the cross I can find my way home from there.

In a confused world, with a lot of splinter groups and confusion, and this philosophy and that trying to solve the problems of a needy world, Jesus says, "Ye are the salt of the earth" (Matt. 5:13). Let Christ live in your life. Be a lighthouse, be a witness. Dare to be different, let your colors be shown. Let the side that you are on be recognized. Be first for Christ. When the world sees the cross, when it sees the Bible, when it sees the Christ, when it sees him living in our lives, then and only then can this needy world find its way home from there. God, help us. Let's be that kind of a church. Let's be that kind of people.

9
The Glorification
of the Believer

"And we know that all things work together for good for them that love God, to them who are the called together according to his purpose. For whom he did fore-know, he also did predestinate to be conformed to the image of his Son, that he might be the firstborn among many brethren. Moreover whom he did predestinate, them he also called: and whom he called, them he also justified: and whom he justified, them he also glorified. What shall we then say to these things? If God be for us, who can be against us? Who shall separate us from the love of Christ? Shall tribulation, or distress, or persecution, or famine, or nakedness, or peril, or sword? As it is written, for thy sake we are killed all the day long; we are accounted as sheep for the slaughter. Nay, in all these things we are more than conquerers through him that loved us. For I am persuaded, that neither death, nor life, nor angels, nor principalities, nor powers, nor things present, nor things to come, nor height, nor depth, nor any other creature, shall be able to separate us from the love of God, which is in Christ Jesus our Lord" (Romans 8:28–31, 35–37) .

My subject is the glorification of the believer. By

the glorification of the believer I mean that cataclysmic and climactic zenith toward which my salvation is moving and in which it shall ultimately result.

Every philosophy of life, every ideology, every concept by which man is living today or by which man has ever lived has some goal toward which it moves, something for which it is striving, the best in reality that it has to offer. And I ask you the question, if you continue to live by the way of life that you have been living, if you pursue the road of life that you have been taking, where is it going to end? What is the best that your religion, or your philosophy, or your ideology has to offer? Where does it go? What will glorification ultimately mean to you?

The glorification of the believer is simply this: that God having foreknown me, did predestinate me to be conformed to the image of his Son, and nothing shall separate me from the final accomplishment of that fact. Now, there are people who talk about being saved and losing salvation. They don't know what being saved is. Being saved is not merely conversion. It is not merely the fact that I shall not go to hell. The Bible says that all things work together for good to them that love the Lord, that are the called together according to his purpose. And what God purposes, God completes. What God starts, God finishes. And I cannot imagine that God is going to foreknow me, then predestinate me, then call me, then justify me, then lose out ninety days later somewhere on the road to heaven. Glorification means I have been saved from the penalty of sin. I am being saved from the power of sin; and I will be saved from the very presence of sin, in heaven, like Jesus, with Jesus forever. And the salvation of the soul, the salvation of a life, the fruition and completion, the great apex and zenith toward which conversion is moving ultimately is no reality at all if a man could start and then fall by the way and lose it. "None that cometh unto him," he says, "will I cast out." "My sheep know my voice, they follow me, I know them. I and my Father are one. I shall not lose one." The glorification of the believer is the fifth part of the panorama of salvation.

Now, let's look at it again. God foreknew me, he predestinated me, he called me, he justified me, then he glorified me. Now, let me say to you as a background that it is impossible for a preacher to mention the word predestination without a lot of people getting mentally hung up right there and not getting past that point and never hearing much else of what he says. The Bible does speak of predestination. *Pre* means aforetime, ahead of time. *Destine* to means to decide, to decide ahead of time. But God did not indiscriminately predecide. I believe that the Bible very emphatically teaches that God's predestination is based upon something. Look at it again. "For whom he did foreknow, them he did also predestinate." Foreknew what? Knew how they would choose!

I have three children. One of them likes green beans, two do not. I may or may not offer the green beans to the other two. It is not that I indiscriminately withhold the green beans, but the fact is that I merely know ahead of time they will not accept them anyway. And so I may or may not offer the beans to those children. I believe that those on whom God decides are those that he knows ahead of time will accept him or reject him. God's superior knowledge knows the end from the beginning. You may be sure that if God in his foreordained counsel and wisdom knows you will accept him, you will be given the chance to be saved. But he does more than that. He tells how he gives them the chance. By calling them to be saved.

Those that he knows, he gives the opportunity, he calls. And whom he calls, he justifies. How glorious that a man might stand justified before God. But though his sins are forgiven, even that is not all there is. There is more. There's more, beyond time and tomorrow. That is that we shall ultimately be like him, for we shall see him as he is.

Again I say that every philosophy of life has its idea of glorification. That toward which it moves. That which is the best that it has to offer, the living end, the apex, the goal, the climax, the zenith. And if you get everything that it has, what have you got?

The early Indians worshiped the eagle. They believed that if one was especially blessed of the gods, one day he would come back, reincarnated as the great American bird. And to live and die and live again as an eagle was glorification to the Indian. It was the ultimate. It was their mecca, this was their heaven, this was their best. And if you had everything that their ancient religion taught, then you would be again an eagle. That was the living end. That was it. If you had that, you had it all!

To the Buddhist glorification is something else. The Buddhists believe that if a person lives an especially good life, at the moment of death the Buddhist priestess Kanon will come from heaven and walk the veil with him as he is transported into the next life. To have her walk with you between earth and heaven and life and death, to have her hand in yours for the brief moments that you passed into the next life, this is the best they have. This is their glorification.

The Red Cross people brought ToJo, when in the war prisons in Japan, one of the Red Cross towels shortly before his death. On the bottom of those towels were the words "Cannon bath towels." They over-heard him saying, "Kanon, Kanon, Kanon." They discovered that he was looking at the little label that said, "Cannon." He believed that at the hour of his death the gods had sent the priestess Kanon to him. He believed that he had experienced glorification. He died believing that Kanon would walk with him into the next life. And that is all Buddhism has to offer.

To the Communists glorification is something else. It is simply this: that man would obliterate forever the "myth" of God from the minds of men, establish a materialist utopia, and establish the economic amelioration of humanity. For all men to be equal, not especially good and not especially bad, not especially rich or especially poor, either all bad or all good, for all to be happy or miserable, but at least to be all the same. This is the best that communism has to offer. Glorification to the Communist is the equality of all, whether equally happy or equally miserable.

To the modern teen-ager glorification is something else. When I was a teen-ager, the living end, the epitome, to have it all, was to have a steady date. But now its different. Today, it is to have a steady crowd. It is to have a group. The herd instinct the psychologists call it. The desire to conformity, the desire to be like everybody else. To find security in losing yourself as one of the little boxes all in a row. Today, most of them act alike, talk alike, dress alike, look alike, and are alike. They are a bunch of little paper dolls, all strung out. No individuality, no difference, just one of the gang, one of the herd, finding some kind of funny, frustrated sense of satisfaction in being like everybody else.

To the modern American, glorification is something else. Glorification to most Americans is materialism. To obtain, to possess, to have plenty of money in the bank, a good job, financial security, a color television set, and plenty of sex on the side. When you've got that, you have arrived. You've got everything. Glorification is materialism to Americans.

But what is glorification to the Christian? Let me repeat it again: that God having foreknown me, did predestinate me, to be conformed to the image of his Son, and nothing, but nothing shall separate me from the final accomplishment of that great fact. Let me say it like this. Glorification is ultimately to be like Jesus. "Oh," says the song writer, "to be like him. More like Jesus every day."

It simply means three things. First, it means to be like him in his desires. I don't know about you, but I have more trouble with me than anybody else. And if

I ever get me straightened out, I think I'll straighten everybody else out.

Jesus Christ was the most oppressed, underprivileged, impoverished, minority individual, cursed and despised, ridiculed, persecuted, hated, misunderstood of any man that ever lived. And yet Jesus, who is the final authority on the subject, said of the needs of life, seek first the kingdom of God and all these things will be added unto you. He was the picture of composure, he was the picture of peace, everywhere that he went. I don't think that there ever was as composed, as beautifully oriented an integrated personality as was the king of kings. He defended little children, he defended others, he defended the Word of God, he defended his heavenly Father, he defended his disciples, but he never defended himself. And one day, thank God, when my body has been saved, as my soul has been saved, when Christ who came the first time to redeem the individual, has come the second time to redeem society, when I stand with him, I shall be like him in his desires. Glorification means not only to be like him in his desires, but it means to be like him in his presence. Now, at the right hand of God. Listen. "Eye hath not seen, nor ear heard, neither have entered into the heart of man, the things which God hath prepared for them that love him" (1 Cor. 2:9).

Often people ask, "Why did God go to all that trouble of making other planets if there is no life there?" Well, in the first place, the Bible tells us why. It is simply to reveal his glory, that it might be his handiwork, that men might look at heaven and see the work of God and praise Him. But what trouble was it for God to make them? He just said, "Be," and it was. But if all the beauty and symmetry, the balance and the wonder of it all, the beautiful planets and universe came into existence simply by one instantly spoken word of his mouth, what is heaven that he's been working on for two thousand years going to be like?

"Eye hath not seen, nor ear heard, neither have entered into the heart of man, the things which God hath prepared for them that love him" (1 Cor. 2:9).

The glorification of the Christian is to be like him in his desires, to be like him in his presence, and thirdly, it is to be like him in his glorified body. A body that cannot sin, a body that cannot lust, a body that is not lazy, a body that cannot be sick, that is not susceptable to hunger and pain, disappointment, poverty, and disease. He came out of the grave in a glorified body, a perfect body, and the Bible says we shall be like him. We too, shall have a glorified body.

Years ago a little girl with a twisted ugly body came home from her first day of school where the other children had mercilessly made fun of her. She crawled up into her mother's lap and asked, "Mamma, why did God make me like this?" And the dear mother with a tear on her cheek and a lot of wisdom in her heart said, "Darling, God's not through making you yet." Hallelujah!!! Oh, to be like him in his body, a glorified body, complete, right, whole before God.

Whichever road of life you choose, I want to ask you if you go as far as it goes, and get all that it offers, what will you have? And it all adds up to one big zero. All but the glorification of the believer, the ultimate end toward which all of Christendom is moving in the plan and purpose of God.

God having foreknown me, did predestinate me to be conformed to the image of his Son, and nothing but nothing shall separate me from the ultimate reality and completion of that final fact.

Years ago a missionary came home from Africa. There at the dock was a brass band and a large crowd. His heart was thrilled. But as they came on board it was to meet a noted politician who was returning home from an African hunting expedition. They put the politician in the back seat of a great car and rode him through a downtown parade. The poor missionary went to a third-story cold-water flat on the east-side of the Bronx. He said he got down on his knees and began to pray, feeling very, very sorry for himself. Flinging himself across the bed, he said, as all of us have done a time or two in our lives, that he began to bawl out the Lord. "Lord, what kind of justice is this. This politician's been off blowing money and having a big time, and he comes home to all of this. I've buried my life in the jungles of Africa for twelve years for you, and I've come home to nothing." He said as he began to wipe away the tears and his heart got quiet and he began to hear the voice of God, the dear Lord said to him, "Son, you haven't come home yet!"

What is it going to be like when we will be with Jesus when we will see him as he is, when we come home? We shall be conformed to the image of his Son. That is the living end! That's the apex! That's the zenith, that is the ultimate toward which Christianity moves for the believer. And you can have it. And if you do not know him as your Savior, I submit to you that the devil is deceiving you and leading you up a blind alley, only to wake up too late one day.

Open your heart and let him in. Jesus will be your dearest friend. He may not pass your way again. Open your heart and let him in.

Other Broadman Books by
John R. Bisagno

The Power of Positive Evangelism. Nashville: Broadman Press, 1968.
The Power of Positive Living. Nashville: Broadman Press, 1969.